FALL ON YOUR KNEES

BURIAL AT THE NATIVITY

BURNING BRIDGE PUBLISHING

FALL ON YOUR KNEES

BURIAL AT THE NATIVITY

as told by Claire Anastas
as told to Danger Geist

www.BurningBridge.com

Copyright © 2022 by Danger Geist

Book art and cover designed by Trevor Niemann
Burning Bridge Publishing logo designed by Ryan Rizzio
Cartography by Mapping Specialists, Ltd.

All rights reserved. No part of this publication may be reproduced, distributed, or transmitted in any form or by any means, except for personal use, and only if content is unaltered and properly credited. All persons and companies are strictly prohibited from gaining any kind of monetary profit from the solicitation of this publication. All inquiries (including mass order pricings) are to be directed to Burning Bridge Publishing.

www.BurningBridge.com

The Burning Bridge Publishing name and logo are trademarks of Burning Bridge Publishing.

Printed in the United States of America.

1st edition, December 2022

Publisher's Cataloging-in-Publication Data

Names: Anastas, Claire, author. | Geist, Danger, author.
Title: Fall on your knees : burial at the nativity / as told by Claire Anastas, as told to Danger Geist.
Description: Tulsa, OK: Burning Bridge Publishing, 2022.
Identifiers: LCCN: 2022921399 | ISBN: 978-1-937691-10-3 (paperback) | 978-1-937691-11-0 (epub) | 978-1-937691-13-4 (Kindle)
Subjects: LCSH Anastas, Claire. | Christians--West Bank--Bethlehem--Biography. | Palestinian Arabs--West Bank--Bethlehem--Biography. | Bethlehem--Religious life and customs. | Bethlehem--Ethnic relations. | Palestine--Politics and government. | Children--Death--Biography. | BISAC BIOGRAPHY & AUTOBIOGRAPHY / Cultural, Ethnic & Regional / Arab & Middle Eastern | BIOGRAPHY & AUTOBIOGRAPHY / Personal Memoirs
Classification: LCC DS110.B4 .A63 2023 | DDC 956.94/2--dc23

for Mirna

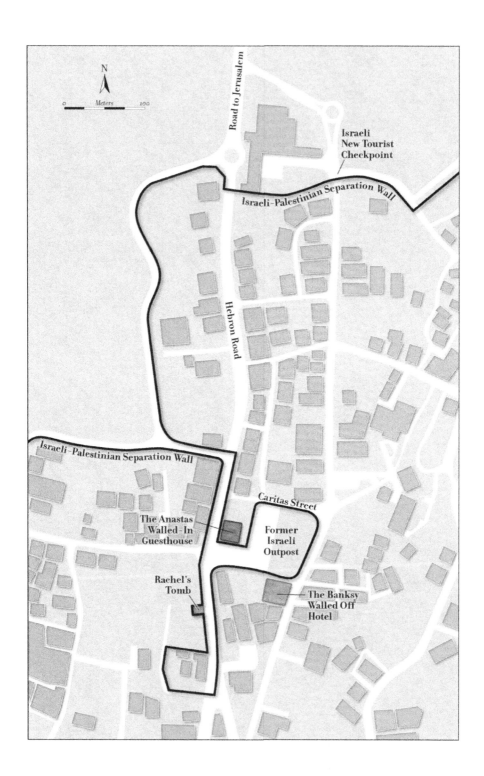

FALL ON YOUR KNEES
BURIAL AT THE NATIVITY

<u>October 8, 1967</u>

The white flag sat atop the Teekay household. The war was over, and they'd lost. Four months prior, bodies had piled across the West Bank, 20 Palestinians for every Israeli. A sweeping victory for their enemies, a generational setback for Arabs. Even still, the Teekays had never wanted anything to do with the violence in the first place. They'd accepted their defeat: the Palestinians lost, and – yes, life was about to change – but they had no intentions of resisting the Israeli presence that now swarmed Bethlehem.

"Umi," Abi Teekay addressed his wife, "I hate to say it, but we need to cook something. Everybody's sick of eating olives and dates."

Umi sighed.

"I know it, too. The kids have been whining for something real to eat."

"You, especially, need to eat," Abi says, then nodded towards her womb. "Of all our problems, I will not allow a malnourished baby to be one of them."

Umi rubbed her belly, then nodded.

"What a curse," Abi lamented, "that we would have all the ingredients to fix a gourmet meal, but can use none of it!"

"It's not a curse. We are blessed beyond measure. Let me go cook some noodles; God will provide the rest for us."

"*The rest*? We already have the food; it is simply safety from Israeli punishment we need."

"Then that is what He will provide, Abi."

Umi smiled, which forced Abi into a wide smile too. She glanced at her four children, and they're giggling at the way their mommy is looking at them. Umi always had a way of making everyone feel buoyant, even in the direst circumstances.

Umi gently shut the door, leaving the room and her smile behind her as she tiptoed up the stairs. She wondered if it would be better to clamor so that the Tzahal would know that she's not a threat. After all, no sniper would be clumsy enough to draw that kind of attention to himself. But being so close to the heels of the Six Day War, Umi knew the Tzahal doesn't differentiate between competent snipers and inept ones.

She opted to keep it nimble and snuck into her kitchen. She threw some water on a pot, and while she waited for it to boil, she peeked at the world outside the window. She could see the stairwell that leads up to the famed Milk Grotto, the location that Mary, Youseph, and Yasue hid after Herod the Great ordered the execution of all male babies in Bethlehem. Now nearly 2000 years later, the Teekays were finding refuge in its neighboring space, praying for protection from the Tzahal.

Today, tourists visit by the daily, many believing that the Grotto grants fertility to couples who visit and pray for children. Legend has it that a drop of the Virgin Mary's milk fell to the floor while feeding Yasue, consecrating the space into a sanctum that reverses infertility. Umi laughed to herself as she considered that maybe her proximity to the Milk Grotto is why she had such success in her own procreation, what with her four children and one on the way now.

But Umi's smile was wiped off of her face as she began to hear an offensive noise.

FWAP. FWAP. FWAP. FWAP.

Umi's heart dropped. She knew the sound.

She froze as the Sikorsky H-34 leveled with her window.

"I'm not a sniper," she muffled to herself, as if the pilot could hear her whisper any better than she could hear herself.

"I'm not a sniper," she yelled at the pilot, waving her arms. "I'm making dinner!"

The chopper remained level with the kitchen, and Umi wondered if her message had been received by the pilot as she hadn't been fired upon yet. But then, she saw the barrels of the affixed guns began to turn.

"I'm not a threat!" she yelled again.

The barrels continued to spin.

Umi threw herself onto the ground as bullets sprayed her kitchen, hitting the pot with such force that it slung onto the floor.

One hand on her belly and one over her head, Umi trembled on the floor until the onslaught ended, the barrels slowed again, and the chopper took off.

"Umi!" Abi roared from downstairs. "Umi! Can you hear me?"

No response.

"Umi!" he yelled for each step he slapped his feet on.

Abi burst through the kitchen door, finding his wife in a pool of blood on the floor.

"I'm fine," Umi calls out. "But the baby..."

"Hush, Umi. Let's get you to the hospital."

"I can't move," Umi wheezed.

"I will carry you," Abi insisted. "Umi..."

"Abi."

"Hold still."

"Abi."

"What is it?"

"Abi, the baby."

Abi looked under her skirt and past the pool of blood to find the baby had been delivered to a world so cruel, she had never been given the opportunity to cry as babies ought to do.

The baby lain on the ground, unconscious, choked to death in her own mother's blood.

<u>October 8, 1967</u>

"She won't make it to the hospital," Abi spoke into the phone's mouthpiece. "We need a doctor to come here. Please. Yes, she's alive and conscious and... what? No. The baby? No. The baby isn't breathing; she's dead. My wife will be soon too if you don't send someone. Yes, Tzahal has gone already."

"Abi, is everyone okay downstairs?" Umi asked in a haze, her blood having already dried on the tile.

"Yes, dear Umi. You should know, we have lost the baby."

"Well," Umi said as a tear rolled down her cheek, "let the doctor determine that."

They didn't have to wait long as the doctor was kneeling before them a few minutes later.

"You have not been shot?" the doctor asked as he listened to the stethoscope on Umi's chest.

"No. I was able to get down very fast," she said, then looked at the breathless baby nearby. "Too fast."

"Well, your heart rate is barely above average and your breathing is not as high as I would expect," the doctor said, then placed the stethoscope on the baby. "Let me check the child."

"She is dead," Abi reassured the doctor.

The doctor didn't respond, his bushy eyebrows concealing his eyes. Until he looked up at Abi without tilting his head and let out a soft, "hmmm."

"'*Hmmm*?'" Abi asked.

"The child is not gone," the doctor explained.

Abi's eyes widened and Umi's face turned from agony to joy.

"But," the doctor tempered their excitement, "she will be dead soon. Her soul will leave her body within two hours."

"What can we do?" Umi asked.

"We must send for the priest."

"The priest?" Abi questioned.

"If you want her to be allowed into the Catholic cemetery with your ancestors, she needs a Christian Baptism."

"As Yasue Messiah entered the world in this manger," Abi said, gesturing his arm to the nearby church that was built upon the spot of Christ's birth, "so our daughter will leave it. We will contact the Church of the Nativity without delay."

October 9, 1967

"The child's name?" the priest asked as he dipped his hands into a portable baptismal font he brought to the house.

"Claire," Umi responded, now lying down on her bed. "Claire Ibrahim."

The priest took Claire into his arms, and pressing her against his chest with his left arm, dipped his right hand into the font and sprinkled water over her forehead.

"Claire Ibrahim Teekay, I baptize you in the name of the Father, of the Son, and of the Holy Ghost."

Umi sobbed. Abi comforted. Claire smiled, then breathed – what felt as if was her first actual breath. And suddenly, she began to breathe consistently. Breathe normally.

"This baby isn't going to die," Umi said.

"She's... lost a lot of blood, Father," Abi whispered to the priest, who nodded.

"My dear," the priest said as he put his hand on Umi's shoulder and explained, "this has all been a very overwhelming experience, and it is good that she breathes on her own now, but you should know that this doesn't mean that she is going to live."

Abi covered his mouth with his hands and nodded, then met the priest's gaze.

"Take heart," the priest said, "she will be buried among the first martyrs."

Hearing this, Abi broke down and wept. The priest's pronouncement needed no explanation: Abi knew the "first martyrs" referred to the infants killed by Herod the "Great" when the king ordered the massacre of the innocents. The Grotto of the Holy Innocents was a chapel underneath the Church of the Nativity, adorned with skulls believed to be from those very children who were murdered in search of the Christchild. Of course Claire would not be buried in the cave itself, but the cemetery was in such proximity to the hallowed grotto that it was surely an honor to rest there.

"She will not die," Umi repeated herself. "Do you understand?"

"There is a shop off Hebron," the priest said, ignoring Umi and placing his hand upon Abi's. "I will give you the address. It is a special shop, a woodworking shop which makes baby-sized coffins. I suggest you visit there. Do not tarry."

Abi took all of his children – save for Claire – and fetched the coffin as the priest instructed. He returned home with a small pine crate, but five hours later, the child had not yet died, so he sent again for the doctor. When the doctor arrived, he was met with a rude welcome.

"You fool!" Abi yelled, clutching the doctor's collar. "You said she'd die and it wasn't worth it to bring her to the hospital! We could have saved her with your medical equipment, but now she will die because of you!"

The doctor threw his hands up, knocking off Abi's hand.

BURIAL AT THE NATIVITY

"Let me through," the doctor said. "I want to see the girl."

The doctor knelt between the casket and the baby, then pulled out his stethoscope and began his assessment. After a few minutes, the doctor closed his eyes and lowered his head, then asked, "what have you done to this girl?"

"What have I done?" Abi said indignantly. "What have *you* done! What have..."

"She is completely healthy," the doctor interrupted Abi.

"What did you say?" asked an incredulous Abi.

"This child: she doesn't need to go to the hospital. She would be the healthiest baby on the wing."

Abi's jaw dropped and he looked over at his wife.

Umi was smiling.

So was her daughter.

FALL ON YOUR KNEES

December 10, 1987

"Abi," 20-year-old Claire asked upon entering her father's factory, "where is Riad's order? He's demanding it. They're saying that we promised it be done today."

"Oh, Riad," Abi chuckled. "You can tell that silly man that I had his order ready for him yesterday, if he really wants to know. His order is in the second cabinet, dear, third from the left."

"Thank you," Claire said, patted Abi on the cheek with a kiss, then left the factory and entered the shop, where Riad stood.

"My father sends his kindest regards," Claire said to Riad as she reached into the second cabinet.

"Is that why he sent a woman to do his work?" Riad asked with a smirk.

"He is very busy today. And Abi is a very good man, dear. He gave me a wonderful childhood. And unlike many of the men in Bethlehem," Claire taunted, "he treats me and my mother with respect."

"But is he an insurgent?" a voice called out from the corner of the room, startling Claire.

A man emerged. He was in a green uniform that bore the Star of David on its sleeve.

"Oh, goodness, I didn't see you standing there," Claire said to the officer, who smiled.

"I'll be on my way," Riad said. "Thank you for crafting this."

"What is this shop that you run here?" the officer asked Claire, eyeing Riad as he left.

"Sir, this is my father's shop. We sell Mother of Pearl here."

"Mother of Pearl?"

"Yes," Claire said, handing the officer an iridescent rosary. "As in, nacre. Mollusk shell."

"I see," he rasped while examining the prayer beads. "And what is it that you do exactly? Do you just work here?"

"I just graduated from school."

"High school, then?"

"College."

The officer was taken aback.

"What did you study? *Mother of Pearl?* With a minor in mollusk?"

"Business," Claire wryly responded. "I am *educated*; not an employee here. I'm helping my father manage this shop while I can."

"Very nice. And your father, does he pay his taxes?"

"I... I suppose so. I'm sure he pays what he owes. But sir, if I may say, if he is late on his taxes, it is only because your country has increased the price of our materials."

"Have we?" the officer asked as he raised his eyebrow.

"Yes. I will not be coy: the basic materials cost five times as much here in Bethlehem than they do in Jerusalem. It is destroying our economy. But that being said, we still pay our taxes."

"That is good. And you're sure that your father pays his taxes?"

"I have said so. I have confidence in him, yes."

"And are you sure that your father isn't a rebel?"

"No!"

As the officer tilted his head, Claire added, "I mean, no, he's *not* a rebel."

"I only ask because there are rumblings that an uprising is coming. Three Palestinians were killed in Jabalia a couple days ago. Purely an accident. But the Palestinians in Gaza do not see it as such, and there has been some violence. We don't want that here; not in this city of Bethlehem, the birthplace of one of your greatest prophets."

"Yasue? Yasue is not a prophet," Claire corrected him. "Yasue is the Christ, the Messiah that your people long-awaited."

The officer was taken aback by her words.

"Do you see what you are still holding?" Claire asked the man, who turned his attention to his hands. "That is a cross. I am a Christian."

"The point still stands, we don't want violence here in the West Bank. But they say that there may be an intifada, like the Iraqis and the Egyptians before them. And we know the intifada worked out for them, but I can assure you that you will not have the same result."

"Sir," Claire became stern, "I don't want any part of violence in Bethlehem. Neither does my father. You won. We lost. We're at peace with it."

"And I have peace to hear that," the officer said. "I must be going, but I will report that this house will not be a problem. And we are all grateful for that."

"As are we. We don't want trouble."

"Do you mind if I take this?" the officer asked, holding up the rosary.

Claire dared not ask why a Jew would want a Christian artifact.

"It is yours," she said.

"Thank you. I will also take this jewelry, please," the officer said as he grabbed three sets of earrings from the counter. "And I thank you for your hospitality."

April 17, 1988

Several months passed since that day the officer visited Abi's shop. The officer's apprehension about an uprising taking place in Bethlehem were realized, and the city had been in upheaval for years. Civil unrest had claimed the lives of dozens of Israelis and hundreds of Palestinians as a long-standing cold tension was finally eclipsed with bloodshed.

But for Claire, the intifada felt as if it was on a separate worldly plain: several months ago, she had married Zuji Anastas, a master mechanic who was well-respected in Bethlehem, a man who knew how to love Claire as her own father had.

"My mother started having children when she was very young, too," Claire beamed at Zuji, sitting at her kitchen table.

"Then it's settled," Claire's young husband said. "We can only hope that we will be blessed with many children to come."

"No, Zuji," Claire corrected her new husband. "We can do more than hope: we can pray. God decides who has children, not us."

Zuji put his hand on Claire's shoulder, and as if he had been waiting for the opportunity for such a punchline, said, "It helps that you grew up next to the Milk Grotto."

Claire covered her mouth as if her laughter would dribble down her chin as her tea would, gasping "Oh, dear Zuji!"

KNOCK. KNOCK. KNOCK.

"Claire!" a voice outside of the house called for her. "Please open up! It's an emergency!"

Claire's eyes furrowed as she looked at Zuji in desperation, then responded to the voice, "Come in, Abi! It's open!"

"Claire!" Abi barged through the door with Umi and Claire's sister. "It's your brother; he's been arrested."

"No," Zuji gasped, his mouth hanging open.

"Who?" asked Claire. "Which one?"

"Walad."

"What did he do?" asked Claire. "What could he do? He's just a boy."

Indeed, Walad was only 15 years old.

"There were some Palestinian boys," Abi explained. "They were throwing stones at the Tzahal who were on a patrol."

"No! Why were they provoking the Tzahal?"

"Why do boys do anything? They were protesting, I guess. The Tzahal began to chase them, and the boys turned a corner and got away – slipping right past Walad. When the Tzahal turned the corner, they only saw Walad standing there with his backpack; the boys had escaped. So they arrested him."

"Well, did they search him?" Zuji asked. "If he was involved, he would have also had a mask or some dirt on his hands."

"They searched him and found nothing," Abi explained. "But do facts matter in these evil times? They needed someone to blame, so they took him."

"Where is he?" Claire stood up. "We can figure out a way."

"We don't even know where he is," Abi said, collapsing in the chair at her kitchen table and holding his head up with two fingers. "And they don't just let visitors in. You know how long the prison lines are; everybody is looking for their loved ones. It would take us three or four days for each prison we try to visit. And he could be at any of the prisons by now."

"So we search for him," Umi chimed in. She was met with blank stares, but the silence merely meant that everyone agreed with her. "It's the only way we'll find him. We split up."

"Yes," Abi broke the silence. "Walad needs us. Before it's too late."

April 18, 1988

Claire rushed into her parents' home, but tiptoed once she reached the kitchen, sensing the aridity of the room. Umi had tears in her eyes, and Abi squinted at the salt shaker as if it was 100 kilometers away.

"You found him?" Claire sat at the table and whispered to Abi as if sharing a secret.

" Okhti did," Abi said, nodding towards Claire's sister.

Silence ensued. Claire couldn't stand it though, and asked, "where was he?"

"Ktzi'ot," Okhti said. "Just in the Negev."

"He... is well?" asked an apprehensive Claire, knowing full well that she wouldn't like the answer.

"He is not," Okhti responded. "He has been tortured."

"How..." Claire began to ask a question, only to be interrupted by Okhti.

"He is missing his fingernails."

Claire's eyes widened.

"His bed sheets," Okhti continued with candor, "they look as if a thousand roses were crushed and smeared upon them."

Claire asked between her weeping, "What can we do?"

"There is nothing to be done," Abi reasoned. "It is up to him now."

"He won't sign a confession," Okhti explained. "They said they would release him if he would just admit that he was throwing rocks at the Israelis."

"So, he does that thing!" Claire insisted, as if Walad could hear her.

"He won't; I tried," Okhti said. "He prefers being tortured than to lie about this. I told him, 'Stop being so proud,' and he said it wasn't about pride, that it was about justice. That it would be wrong for him to admit to something he didn't do."

"So what can we do?" Claire asked again.

"There is nothing we can do," Abi said with a twinge of anger. "God has laid out the path for Walad. He will be like the prophets and the apostles; they all were imprisoned too."

"Maybe after the insurgency is over, they will release him," Umi said, trying to add an optimistic quality to the conversation.

"Maybe," Abi said, nodding his head.

March 4, 1990

"I love you," Claire cooed at her baby. "Yes, I do, dear."

"Not so long ago," Abi said with a smile, "I was cooing at you the way you're cooing at Ebnahty."

"What a wonderful legacy you've imprinted on the world," Claire told Abi. "Your name will be remembered for generations now."

"I don't need history to remember me," Abi said, "so long as you do."

"Abi," Claire's sister, Okhti, interrupted, "there is a young man wandering towards our house."

"Oh," Abi replied, still only interested in Ebnahty.

"He looks very dirty. His clothes don't fit. And he's coming right towards us."

Abi jumped from his chair to investigate.

"What is that man doing?" Abi asked as he looked out the window. "He looks drunk. Far be it from me to allow any more trouble to befall this household. Okhti, shoo him away."

As Okhti approached the man, Umi, Abi, and Claire gathered by the window, their breath fogging the window.

"Abi, breathe softer!" Umi demanded.

The three of them watched as Okhti approached the man. After a terse exchange, Okhti threw her arms around the man and began to weep.

"What has that man done to her?" Abi asked, then jettisoned to Okhti. Claire followed after handing Ebnahty to Umi.

"What is going on here?" Abi asked as Okhti continued to hold the man in an embrace.

"Abi," the young man crooned. "Do you not recognize your own son?"

"Walad!" Abi cried as he tossed his arms around both Walad and Okhti.

"Brother," a stunned Claire said as she examined Walad. He had gone from pre- to post-pubescent, now tall and lanky with a deep voice. He had cut the sides of his pants so he could fit into them, and his shirt was too short to cover his belly. It was the same clothes he had been arrested in.

"How did you..."

"They released me this week. I hitchhiked across the Negev Desert. It's not so tough for people to have pity on you when your hands are covered in bandages."

Walad unwrapped his coral-stained dressing and revealed that he no longer had fingernails on either hand.

"They will grow back," Abi enthused. "Six months from now, all will be restored – including those nails. Come, let's get you something to eat and some new clothes. Let's celebrate! We are a family again!"

Yes, they were a family again. But the family unraveled before Walad had his fingernails back.

May 6, 1990

Silent night. Claire and Zuji and their baby, Ebnahty, all slept peacefully, despite the insurgency intensifying each week. Two months is what the Teekays were gifted with: it had been two months since Walad's return home from prison, and despite the political tension in Bethlehem, Claire's world felt like a utopia for that entire time. Her assumption was that this peace would last, that God was restoring all things around her right before her eyes.

Two months. And then it arrived, the Teekays none-the-wiser that their final hour of peace had passed off into the night breeze as Claire woke up to a clatter.

"Zuji," Claire said as her eyes widened. "Zuji, what was that noise?"

"Mmmm," Zuji groaned.

"Zuji, something just happened very close to us."

"Yes," Zuji groaned again, still not moving. "The wind is making lots of loud noise tonight."

Then screaming.

Zuji popped up in bed to listen again.

Another scream.

"The wind does not scream," Claire said, putting her shoes on and flying out the door to see the commotion.

In the dead of night, Claire quickened outside to find her two brothers, Shaqiq and Akhi, in handcuffs, surrounded by seven Tzahal. Umi was clutching Shaqiq, screaming as a soldier pried her apart from her son.

"They have not done what you think they have!" Abi protested to the Tzahal.

"This is what you say," the Samal noted. "Why don't your children speak for themselves?"

"We have spoken!" Akhi said. "You do not tell us why we are being arrested! Whatever you think we have done..."

The Samal smacked Akhi on the head, then the Tzahal stuffed Shaqiq and him into their humvee.

"Please," Abi pled. "At least tell us why you arrest my sons."

"We know about the meetings," the Samal replied. "There are young men at your house every night."

"None of this is as you say!" Abi shouted with tears in his eyes. "I know nothing about young men at my house."

"You may not know," the Samal said, then nodded at the men in the humvee, "but they know. They host these meetings to recruit youth to the insurgency."

"Sir, if there were meetings like this in my home, I would know," Abi restated. "It is not as you say it is."

"You know how this works," the Samal cut through Abi's pleading. "I have my orders."

"How long will my sons be in prison?" Abi asked.

"I know not," the Samal replied, then added, "Maybe you can ask Yitzhak."

<u>September 23, 1990</u>

"It seems every time we are gaining a child through you," Abi observed to Claire, "we lose another to the Tzahal. This time, you must be having twins."

"It will need to be twins if I'm ever to catch up to Umi," Claire said, stroking her *very* pregnant belly. It caused Abi to smile, something Claire hadn't seen him do in the three months since Akhi and Shaqiq were arrested.

"With Ebnahty, you couldn't even tell you were pregnant. Now, well... it seems that perhaps there really are two or three in there."

"No," Claire laughed. "It is only one, and her name will be Mirna. It means 'peace,' and peace we will have."

"Peace we will have," Abi repeated.

Then, a gentle knock at the door. Abi checked the peephole, and his eyes drooped as if weighed down.

"It is the Tzahal again."

Abi opened the door, then said, "hello," as if he was exhaling for the first time in hours. Abi noticed the soldier's rank: a Samal, same as the one who took Akhi and Shaqiq.

"Good morning," the Samal said. He was much softer-spoken than the one that had come in the middle of the night. "I am here to inform you about your son."

"Inform me of wha...," Abi gasped, not even able to finish his sentence.

"You will see your son this week."

"Shaqiq and Akhi?" Abi asked. "They are released?"

"Akhi is coming home. He would not admit to the crime, and there is no evidence against him."

"Why not Shaqiq? Shaqiq is just as innocent as Akhi, just as innocent as anyone in this house."

"He admitted to his crime," the Samal said.

"This is not possible," Abi said. "He is not guilty! Surely if you know Akhi is not guilty, you also know Shaqiq is not either."

"I did not say Akhi is not guilty," the Samal corrected Abi. "I said we do not have evidence against him. For Shaqiq, a confession is evidence enough."

"Sir," Claire cut in, "the only reason Shaqiq would confess to a crime he did not commit is if you tortured him. So I suppose you helped him sign his confession, given that he probably doesn't have any fingernails left?"

Claire and the Samal locked eyes, exchanging contempt for one another. Abi, sensing the increasing tersity, thanked the Samal for the message and shut the door.

And then Abi collapsed into his chair and began crying.

Claire rubbed her father's back and said, "I am so sorry, dear."

Abi stood back up, forced a smile, and announced through his tears, "This is a good day. Let us plan for a big meal."

"Okay, we shall do that very thing," Claire agreed.

"Akhi is coming home, and it is a good day," Abi murmured as if he was only speaking to himself now. He nodded, then repeated his mantra.

"It is a good day."

September 24, 1990

"Claire," Umi called as she gently shook her daughter awake. "Claire..."

"Umi? What time is it?"

"It is 3:00am. And your father has grown sick."

"Sick? What's wrong, Umi?"

Umi maintained a stoic expression, not answering her question, so Claire repeated herself.

"What is wrong, dear Umi?"

Holding back tears, Umi said, "You must go see Abi now."

Claire got up, got dressed, and staggered across the street to her parents' home, where she knocked as she entered.

"Abi?" she said. "Abi? It is Claire. May I come in?"

Claire looked behind herself; Umi hadn't followed her home.

"Abi? I am coming in to see you," she said, then passed the threshold into his quarters.

"Abi?"

She approached her father's bed and found him lying face down in his pillow.

"Abi," she said, beginning to shake him awake.

He wasn't waking. He was stiff and his face had grown cold.

"Abi!"

She began shaking frantically, trying to wake her father.

"He passed away," Umi said through her tears, appearing behind Claire. "I think he had a heart attack. I didn't want to startle you because of your pregnancy; I wanted you to see for yourself."

Claire grew dizzy as she began to hyperventilate.

"I think I," she started to say as she stumbled around the room. "I think. I think I, just..."

In a moment too fast for Umi to catch her daughter, Claire crashed to the ground.

"Claire!" Umi cried, falling to her daughter's side. "Wake up! Please wake!"

Claire remained unconscious. And from under her daughter's gown, Umi could see blood pooling on the floor.

<u>September 24, 1990</u>

"He's gone!" Claire wailed on her hospital bed. "Dear Abi has departed us all!"

"Claire, you must calm," Umi pleaded through her own tears. "It is as they said: the baby will suffer too if you don't calm."

Claire wept into her pillow as a doctor entered the room.

"My name is Dr. Saad, and I think we can save your baby."

"Mirna," Claire corrected Dr. Saad.

"Mirna?"

"That is the child: Mirna. And peace we will have."

"We can save Mirna, I think. It was good that you got here so quickly. We will keep you here so we can continue to monitor you, probably until the baby comes."

"Now that I'm in labor, when will the baby come?"

"You are not in labor. You are weeks away, in fact. I think we will keep you here for about a month, maybe more."

"No," Claire shook her head. "Abi's funeral will be very soon; I must be with the family as we prepare for that. Far be it that you would have equip me with a johnny gown that be black! I wish to be with my family for the 40 days."

Dr. Saad knew the practice of mourning for 40 days. It mattered not if Claire was Muslim or Christian, for every religious Arab had attached significance to the 40th day after death. The belief goes that a recently departed soul must wander the earth for 40 days before judgment, just as the Dajjal will roam the world for 40 days and 40 nights, or just as Moses waited upon Mt. Sinai for 40 days and 40 nights to receive the Law, or just as Yasue fasted for 40 days and 40 nights before ascending the Mount of Temptation, or just as any of the other 37 examples in these sacred texts that emphasize the number 40.

"I understand how important that must be to you," Dr. Saad reasoned with Claire, "but you need to stay in the hospital or your baby will not survive."

"Dear sir," Claire reasoned back, "we must have faith."

"Claire, faith does not give us the excuse to be reckless. You have lost too much blood; your child needs you to rest."

"When I was born, the doctor said I would not survive, but he turned out to be a hindrance. Now you say Mirna will not survive, and you are being that hindrance now."

Dr. Saad sighed.

"Claire, please. Your umbilical cord is compressed, maybe even prolapsed. You need constant care. Mirna needs constant care."

"Doctor," Claire said as she whipped her legs over her bedside, "it's time for me to go. I have daily liturgies to attend to for my father. Thank you for your help."

"*Please*, Claire. Do not let your religion be the reason for more unnecessary suffering."

She was no longer in the mood for negotiating.

"Release me."

September 26, 1990

The Church of the Nativity looked more like a black sea than a place to celebrate the location of the Christchild's birth: everyone in attendance was wearing dark colors, mirroring their dark emotions as they gathered to mourn Abi.

Claire, wearing a black dress and black bonnet, kept looking over her shoulder as she sat at the front.

"They'll be here," Zuji reminded Claire.

"You trust the Tzahal too much. I don't think they'll get their release. Even if they do, as soon as they show up, we must get started."

Zuji nodded. To this, he agreed with Claire. The Tzahal agreed to let Akhi and Shaqiq be released, but only for 30 minutes – even though a traditional Catholic funeral usually eclipses the one-hour mark. After those 30 minutes were up, Akhi would have to go back to the Negev Desert to serve his final two days before his release, and Shaqiq would have to go back to serve the remainder of his term.

Claire heard a commotion at the back of the church and whipped her head around to see her brothers drifting down the aisle. They were dirty; still wearing their bright pink jumpsuits and mud-laden boots.

Claire jumped out of her seat, hastened to them, and wrapped her arms around their necks as they all sobbed together.

Abi was given a beautiful – and full, hour-long – Mass, with even the Mayor of Bethlehem saying a few words. After the Mass ended, Shaqiq and Akhi stood up and gave Claire a warm embrace.

"I am sorry this happened to you," Claire whispered to her brothers. "First they took Walad, and now they wrongfully imprison you. Shaqiq, we will fight until the day you are proven innocent."

"Yes," Shaqiq said, shifting his eyes around the room. "Walad was indeed innocent."

Claire felt it a particularly curious statement for her brother to make. She looked over to Akhi to see if he also felt the comment was bizarre, but he was squarely staring at the marble floor.

"Walad was innocent," Claire reiterated, then posed a second statement that turned into a question by the time she was finished saying it. "And you both are also innocent…"

Akhi did not move his hanging head, still staring at the ground.

"*Akhi*," Claire gasped. "*Shaqiq*. Please tell me…"

"This *isn't* to be discussed right now," Shaqiq replied. "These walls have ears. You know this."

"So," Claire said while rubbing her face, almost gouging her eyes. "Did Abi know?"

"No," Akhi snapped back in a loud whisper. "*No*. He had no idea. That had nothing to do with what happened to him. Listen, Claire. They took Walad from us for years. *For years!* They stole his childhood. You see how it has grieved him so! And you expect us to do nothing about it?"

"You're right," Claire said, "this is not the place for this."

"Don't tell Umi," Shaqiq appealed of Claire.

"And lose her too?" Claire snapped back. "I have been robbed of my whole family, save for her. You must go serve your sentences. I want nothing to do with this."

Shaqiq and Akhi retreated to the back of the church, but instead of finding their Israeli officer, there was the mayor. The brothers nodded at the mayor and then began to leave the church, but the mayor slapped his hand across each of their chests.

"Stay."

"It is not our decision to make," Shaqiq explained.

"Believe us," Akhi said, "we would stay if we could."

The mayor closed his eyes, breathed deeply, and shook his head.

"No," the mayor said. "You're not going back. I will take care of this."

The mayor's eyes strained with stern authority.

"You will stay."

September 29, 1990

"Zuji!"

Zuji awoke, sprung from his chair, and rubbed his eyes.

"Claire? Where are you?"

"Zuji!" Claire screamed again from the next room over.

Zuji rushed to the bathroom where he found Claire standing with blood on the floor.

"It's too much blood this time," she said. "We can't ignore this."

Zuji scooped up Claire into his arms and scampered to the hospital, wheezing the whole way until they arrived to the emergency entrance.

"Please," Zuji heaved, "Claire. Labor. *Baby!*"

"Great! Congratulations," the receptionist said. "When is the baby due?"

"Next month," Zuji gasped.

The receptionist's eyes swelled and Claire was ushered onto a rusty gurney and into a placid room with pink walls.

"Claire," Dr. Saad announced himself as he entered the room. "Tell me what's been going on."

"I'm bleeding. It's been happening since I left the hospital last time, but today it's been too much."

Dr. Saad took less than a minute to complete his checkups.

"You are not the one who is bleeding," he announced, before adding, "This will be the fatal wound. I told you this would happen."

"What did you tell me?" Claire clarified.

"Because of you, your daughter will die."

September 29, 1990

In the small Bethlehem hospital, over the ensuing hours as the contraction pangs transformed into dolorous affliction, Claire remained steadfast that Mirna would not be lost.

"Your God may say that she will live, but my god is science," Dr. Saad explained with the bedside manner of a bedside pan. "And science says she will die."

"I woke up to this world nearly drowning in my mother's blood. A doctor from this very hospital said the same as you, that I had no chance of survival. They fetched me a casket instead of a bassinet. My God prevailed against science that day, and you will see Him again today."

"I don't know what happened that day," Dr. Saad asserted, "but what you are facing now is very serious. I think you may have had a velamentous cord insertion or possibly a prolapsed umbilical cord. If not that, then it was certainly placenta previa. You had symptoms of all three abnormalities, and this is why I wanted you in my care last week."

Claire winced in pain, her eyes retreating to the back of her head as she bit her lip and twisted her body. A moment passed, then she recaptured her composure.

"On that day," Claire regressed to the story of her birth, "they said I had lost too much blood, as you say now. But then they baptized me in the Name of the Father, the Son, and the Holy Ghost, and my sickness departed. You will witness this today."

"I wish this for you," Dr. Saad responded, in a rare moment of tenderness. "If it is as you say, that God still works miracles today, then that is what we will require."

Claire smiled for a moment, but then simpered out coiled cries. She fell into agony before her smile even had reached the corner of her lips.

"We can't keep Mirna in there any longer," Dr. Saad declared. "It's time to try to save her life. Breathe, Claire. Breathe."

It was a quick delivery; Mirna wanted to come out, the womb no longer a sustainable haven. She came into the world, coughing her mother's blood while simultaneously having too little blood inside her own tiny, premature body.

Claire held her sweet daughter, and all the pain washed away for a flitting moment.

"I love you," Claire wooed to Mirna as she cradled her.

"I'm sorry, but I need to take her right away," Dr. Saad explained, then carried Mirna over to the counter across the room. He checked for a heartbeat, and only hearing the faintest taps within, shook his crestfallen head.

"I told you!" Dr. Saad roared, allowing his emotions to get the best of him. "I told you this was the outcome!"

"Doctor," the nurse yelled, "something's wrong. She's slipping away."

"Don't you think I can see that?" Dr. Saad retorted as he conducted compressions on Mirna.

"No," the nurse muttered as she put her hand on Dr. Saad's shoulder. "Not the baby."

Dr. Saad whipped his head towards Claire to find she had slipped out of consciousness.

October 6, 1990

SMACK!

Claire jolted awake, a raised, red mark emerging across her face.

"Please, stop doing that," Claire told her mother.

"You are falling back asleep," Umi defended herself. "I don't want you going into another coma."

"I understand, but... can you smack me a little lighter? Or at least on the other cheek? Or perhaps... tickle me?"

"I've been a nurse longer than you've been alive," Umi responded. "And I've been your mother for as long as you've been alive, and I happen to know you'd rather get smacked than tickled."

Claire emitted a soft, terse laugh.

"Maybe," Claire admitted.

"If you fall asleep, they're going to need to give you a blood transfusion."

"Has there been any update on Mirna?"

"No, but it's as they said: no news is good news."

"I suppose," Claire said as she adjusted to her side, facing Umi. "If they're so sure Mirna will die anyway, I wonder why they brought her to the incubator."

"All we can do is have faith now," Umi said as Claire's eyelids again slowly closed.

SMACK!

"Wake up, Claire."

SMACK!

"Claire..."

SMACK!

"Dr. Saad!"

October 8, 1990

"Your daughter is barely hanging on," Dr. Saad said.

"What else can we do?"

"We've done it all. If the blood transfusion didn't help, then it's too late. And I hate to ask this, but given the circumstances, I need to know. If your daughter doesn't make it, and Mirna does, are you prepared to take her in?"

Umi broke down crying, unable to answer the question.

"Dr. Saad," a nurse interrupted. "There's a pr... I would like to talk to you in the other room."

Dr. Saad looked at the nurse as he held his hand on Umi's back.

"It's urgent," the nurse added.

And Umi was left alone with her tears, though she fell asleep even before her tears dried as she sat waiting.

A few hours later, Dr. Saad found Umi slumped over her chair, resting her head on the concrete wall. He gently touched her shoulder, and Umi bounced to her feet as if she was a junior Tzahal who was just caught sleeping on duty by her Samal.

"Dr. Saad."

She looked into his downturned eyes, which seeped of grief. He squeezed her shoulder.

"I'm sorry," Dr. Saad apologized, almost as if he was defending a particularly poor choice to a superior. "Mirna is... sick. Sicker than she should be. We put her in an incubator. But... I didn't know."

Umi removed Dr. Saad's hand from her shoulder and peered into his sad eyes.

"I didn't know... the incubator we put her in, it had not been disinfected. The baby before Mirna... there was a terrible infection. That baby had passed away, but the incubator was never cleaned. Somehow. I don't know how. Mirna has contracted that same infection that killed that child."

"My granddaughter will die because of this?" Umi asked, taking Dr. Saad's hand into her palms.

"Germs – so insidious. Unseen. They swim on surfaces, sail on the air. Innocuous, they loll on a fomite, and then they die, unless they find a host. Unless they make their way into a vulnerable throat, then the virus attaches. Multiplies itself. The immune system fights it, forgetting its top goal: make sure we're breathing. The oxygen can't get through the capillaries, and then it's over."

"How far has the infection progressed?" Umi asked.

"There is no need to be concerned about having to raise Mirna."

October 13, 1990

Her eyes opened. The world was still spinning – too fast for Claire's liking. She saw a figure in the chair, but her vision was blurred and she couldn't decipher the shadow.

"Umi?" Claire inquired.

"They're all gone," a deep voice responded.

"Doctor?" Claire asked.

No response.

Claire scraped her eyes with her nails, and her vision slowly came back. The figure, indeed, was Dr. Saad, who hunched over in the visitor's chair with his head cradled in his hands, still in his bright lab coat.

"Where is Umi?" Claire asked.

"I was wrong," Dr. Saad announced, a defeated man. "My god is no god. I don't know what's worse: not having any chance of saving her, or that we could have saved her and failed to."

"Who?"

"I don't know what's worse, if it be that your God didn't have the power to save, or that your God did have the power to save and refused to save them."

"Who is *them*?" Claire asked, now frustrated at the cryptic man who is normally so straightforward.

"The children, Claire," Dr. Saad said, finally looking up at her with intensely cardinal eyes.

He seemed a different man. His outline was so vivid to Claire, as if a cartoon, and his presence was so cutting that Claire actually felt discomfort.

"What children, doctor? Where is Mirna? And where is my Umi?" Claire asked, slicing into his crimson eyes with her own tensity.

"Umi is on her way to the church to get the priest. Your daughter was afflicted with an infection. A lethal virus. A contagion so communicable that every other baby on the wing was infected. All six of them infected. All six of them dead."

Claire's eyes swelled as her heart sunk.

"All of the babies are gone?" Claire asked.

"All," the doctor shook his head, "but your Mirna."

"Mirna."

"Your God – the God of Moses, who killed hordes of infants at Passover – is alive today. This God – who, in this very city, orchestrated the Massacre of the Innocents to spare one child at the expense of all the others in Bethlehem – He is seemingly here. For only He could compose a symphony so bloodthirsty as this."

"May I see her?"

"Normally, I would not allow it. But there are no more babies for you to kill, and she is going to die anyway."

"No. Not my girl. Not my Mirna."

October 13, 1990

Claire cradled Mirna, but Mirna's throat was too obstructed for her to even cry.

"You only have a few moments left," a young doctor told her as he tracked Mirna's heart with a stethoscope, Dr. Saad having gone home.

"I want you to see what happens when the priest comes back," Claire told the doctor, whose skeptical eyes belied his nodding head.

"Mirna," Claire cooed in her ear, "my little girl. Arise."

Umi rushed into Claire's room, seeing her daughter – and granddaughter – awake for the first time together in days, months, years, lifetimes, or however long ago it was.

"Claire!" Umi yelled, wrapping her arms around her daughter, then acknowledged the priest she brought with.

"Father is going to say a prayer. Well, Baptize. Father is going to Baptize Mirna."

Claire smiled.

"Baptize her, Father, and we will watch as the God of Abraham, Isaac, and Jacob takes away all her pain."

The priest extended his hand, sprinkled water on Mirna's crown, and rubbed his thumb over her forehead as he trumpeted with authority:

"Mirna Anastas, I baptize you in the Name of the Father, of the Son, and of the Holy Ghost."

The room hushed, making way for reverent silence.

Mirna interrupted the quiet with a vociferous gasp, then gurgled as she caught Claire's eyes with her own. Mirna smiled just before her pupils dilated for a brief moment, then shrunk to midposition.

"Mirna," Claire whispered, then put the back of her hand on her daughter's cheek. "She has gone cold. *Help!*"

The doctor felt her cheek, then placed his stethoscope on the middle of her chest. Then just to the left of her thorax. Then to the right. Then he grabbed her tiny wrist and measured her pulse. Then dropped her hand and frantically used his stethoscope to find any sign of life.

The doctor shook his head and unequipped his stethoscope.

"Her heart has stopped," the doctor announced.

October 14, 1990

Claire suffocated her face into her pillow, eyes crusted over and her dried tears so thick that it almost seemed like a goo. Her throat was hoarse and growing sore, both as a result of her screaming at God all night.

"Why, Yasue, why?," she had screamed like a broken record until her head was pounding like an unexpected knock obtruding a deep nap. "It wasn't enough for you to take my father, but you take my daughter too? Why would you do this to one of your faithful servants! Why, Yasue, why?"

That was hours ago, though. Now that she was done screaming, she just whirled about in her mind the image of Mirna smiling at the moment of her death, her baby girl's expression swirling over and over in her memory. Claire was stuck in a mental revolving door that wouldn't offer an exit until the image became plastered into her very being.

Oh, baby girl, my second baby! Did you even know how beloved you were? If each day had been a year, I still would have needed more time with you. Is it that I didn't love enough? How can it be that your blood would be on my own hands? How can the Lord ever restore me now?

The 13th of October, 1990. A Saturday. The same day of the week Mirna was born.

Zuji, too, was tossing and turning, and just as Claire became convinced that neither of them would ever get any sleep again, a shadow entered the bedroom.

Claire sprung up in her bed and shouted, "who's there?"

She turned to Zuji, who was now asleep and unbothered by her loud voice.

Claire squinted at the shadow, and as her eyes adjusted, she saw the shadow was actually quite tall and hovered over the foot of her bed.

"Why did you take away my child?" Claire asked the shadow.

"*Me?*," the shadow said, revealing her voice to be a woman's. "It wasn't *I* who took her away. But you see? She is not gone."

The shadow revealed that she was holding Mirna, who looked to be asleep and her breathing no longer labored, her disposition being one of utter peace.

"Baby..." Claire gasped.

"You have always had visions, haven't you, Claire?" the shadow asked. "Since you were a child, you could see events before they happen, and you'd be able to change the outcomes of bad situations by knowing how they'd end up if you didn't act."

"Yes, you're right," Claire affirmed. "I know how things are going to happen. It changes the way I handle the situation."

"But you didn't see this coming. And you sure wish you could have avoided this, don't you?"

Claire only responded by allowing a single trickle to melt down her cheek.

"A time is coming," the shadow continued, "when these visions will stop. Instead, you will have a Champion by your side at all times. He will tell you what to do in the situations as they happen, and you will trust and know what to do without a moment's notice."

"Okay," Claire said, much more concerned about getting to hold her baby again. "What are you doing with my child?"

"It's time for a bath," the shadow declared, then disrobed Mirna into nakedness and began to disappear into the back of the room.

Claire launched out of bed and cried, "wait," but the shadow held her palm in front of Claire, which Claire respected by stopping her pursuit. Behind the shadow, a candle flickered, revealing a bright white room with a large basin full of water.

"This candle burns for Mirna," the shadow said. "And peace you will have."

Claire peered into the room, and saw the wrinkled face of the woman who had lit the candle: it was her grandmother, who would wake up before dawn each morning and moonily scale hundreds of steps to reach the Church of the Nativity, where she would enter the cave that now hosts the manger scene of Christ. She was devout to her call to follow Christ, all the way until her death several years ago.

"It's not for you to see," the shadow told Claire, then took Mirna into the bath.

Claire's grandmother glanced at Claire, smiled, and the shadow shut the door. As the sanitized room became sealed, Claire felt an inner peace about Mirna's passing, as if Claire could tell that Mirna's time on earth was going to be marked with tragedy and suffering beyond what she could bear, and instead Mirna now would have an eternity of peace instead – even if it took some of Claire's peace on earth in the meantime.

Claire didn't even attempt to open the door again, instead falling to her knees and praying the Lord's prayer over and over.

"Our Father, who art in heaven..."

She prayed so fervently that the words almost seemed as if they weren't even coming from her own mouth, like an entity was controlling her words and simply pouring aloud what had been in her heart. After a few iterations of the prayer, she opened her eyes and found herself back in bed. She looked over and found Zuji finally in a deep sleep.

But she could still hear the Lord's prayer being recited.

"...hallowed be Thy Name. Thy Kingdom come, thy will be done..."

Claire slipped out from the covers and looked out the window to see some kind of prayer vigil outside, where the participants were praying the Rosary.

"Not for me to see," Claire remembered the words from the shadow. "Not yet."

November 26, 1990

Claire buried her daughter among the first martyrs, in the cemetery alongside the Church of the Nativity that had allotted a plot for Claire so many years ago. But this suffering was not, in itself, satisfactory: while mourning Mirna, Claire's backyard was chosen to become the site of an Israeli bivouac. Not only would the Anastas home lose their privacy, but soldiers would be allowed to come in as they please to use their roof for surveillance.

"Your house is plotted on Israeli soil," the Samal explained.

"This is not Israel," Claire blustered at the idea that her enemies would have full access to her house whenever they wanted. "This is Palestine!"

"Palestine *is* Israel," the Samal barked back. "We would not need to do this, but you know full well that your people... that is to say, *some* Palestinians have begun using weapons against us. We don't wish for any of this to be escalated, but we simply cannot have our soldiers being attacked."

"And you cannot choose one of the *many* empty homes on this street?" Claire asked.

"Claire Anastas, your home is three stories tall and provides natural protection from bullets," the Samal reasoned with Claire, even with a hint of empathy. "Does it make you feel better if I tell you that Rachel's Tomb is being commandeered to become a military fortress, too? Your backyard is far from being the only piece on the chessboard, here. If you point to me another house that has three stories with access to a roof like yours, and I promise you, Miss Anastas, we will set up our outpost there instead."

"Is it because we have the best house that you also steal from our shelves?" Claire protested, now airing other grievances she had long bottled up. "Is it because of Saddam Hussein that your junior soldiers' pockets are lined with my mother's pearls?"

"No, we take from your house because you have not paid your tariff," the Samal responded, his voice deepening and becoming much more emphatic than empathic.

"That is not true," Claire boiled. "We have paid every shekel of the 18% you demand from us!"

"Even so, many of you Arabs are not paying your tariff. For some, they pay less than what is due. For others, they pay more to offset what your brothers and sisters fail to give."

"Why do you call them my 'brothers and sisters?' Do you believe that we all live in harmony without our own conflicts? I am a Christian. My heroes are your heroes. I do not receive any support from Arabs who are not also Christian."

"So then, call upon your Christians to help you."

"There are none of us left!" Claire cried.

Indeed, the Samal knew she was not overstating the reality. Bethlehem had seen their own exodus as native Palestinians fled the city in hordes because of the Gulf War. While the war itself was fought well over 1000km away in Iraq and Kuwait, the Iraqi military dared Israel to get involved so that Saddam Hussein would be justified to use chemical weapons on Jerusalem. Like Iraqis, Palestinians are Arabs, and the Palestinian sympathy for their Iraqi counterparts in the east was palpable, often leading to clashes between Palestinian civilians and the Tzahal. In Kuwait, many Arabs were exiling from their homeland and resettling in the West Bank of Palestine, often bringing the war with them and dragging the native Palestinians into the crossfire.

Christians in particular were emigrating in droves as they did not have the support of non-Christian Arabs in Bethlehem: During the Israeli War of Independence, Bethlehem was 85% Christian. By the Six-Day War twenty years later, only 46% of Bethlehem was Christian. A quarter-century later, as Claire stood before the Samal, that number had dwindled to 40% and Christians had officially become the minority in the birth city of Yasue. Even Claire was wrestling with her faith as she slowly became a persecuted people, and for what? To serve a God who would take her peace?

BURIAL AT THE NATIVITY

Of course Claire could not have foreseen it, but in less than 20 years, the Christian population in Bethlehem would nearly tauten to extinction. Surely, pilgrims come and tourists go, but the number of Christians who steadfastly suffer for the cause of Christ in the city of His birth is less than a mere 5% today.

"Well, you must know you're not the only one with this problem," the Samal said, the waning drips of his patience now spilt. "From the dissolution of the Soviet Union, we have Jews fleeing from the northeast and pouring into our borders."

"But you have the support from the strongest country in the world," Claire clapped back. "While Americans have spent their effort throwing their support behind Israel, they have ignored the fact that this support is creating unchecked persecution upon Christian minorities here in Bethlehem."

"We will only be here for a brief moment," the Samal assured Claire. "Can this conflict last forever?"

Laden with grief over the losses of both Mirna and now her backyard, Claire resigned herself to accept that she must sleep with the enemy just outside of her window.

December 2, 1990

Claire woke up on a Sunday morning to the sound of an excavator outside her window. She got out of bed and thumbed the plastic sheet that was over her window to peep outside, just in time to see the excavator dig up her bed of flowers in her backyard.

Usually there were several soldiers congregating in her backyard, but today it was only the excavator and its operator.

Claire checked her watch: a minute after 5:00am. She hustled to the kitchen and threw on a pot of coffee, poured a cup, and met the Turai just before he knocked on the front door.

"Good morning, Chileab," Claire said to her enemy, opening her door and offering him the cup. "Would you like some coffee?"

"Not today," the teenager said, then briskly pushed past Claire and headed to her roof, calling down when he got to the third floor. "But thanks."

"He's cranky today," Zuji said, sneaking up behind Claire and putting his chin on her shoulder.

"Probably because the sun is rising earlier and earlier," Claire said, grabbing Zuji's hand that's wrapped around her waist. "I'm telling you, one of these times, he's going to miss his stand-to, and they will demote him."

"Claire," Zuji laughed, "he is a foot soldier. I don't think a Turai can be downgraded any lower."

"Well, dear, then this is a perfect explanation for why he's so cranky. Coffee?"

Zuji smiled and took the steaming cup, his mustache dipping into the coffee before he returned to his chambers.

Another of the Tzahal – that is, another lowly Turai – tried to sneak out Claire's front door without having to converse with any of the Palestinians in the house, but Claire caught him anyway.

"Moshe?" she said, "how was your shift? Are you not helping Chileab with the sunrise watch?"

Moshe turned around. He was just a teenager, too, though the younger of the two soldiers. Moshe was perhaps not even old enough to legally sip araq. Despite his youth, he had bags under his eyes and almost looked inebriated. He didn't want to be here; it's just part of his mandatory service.

"My shift was fine," he responded, trying to slip away before Claire snuck another question in.

"What are they doing out there?" she asked.

"I... well, this location – your backyard – they have chosen it for a camp."

Claire knew this already. More, the Turai knew that Claire knew this.

"So, I am not allowed to use the front door to leave, and now I must squeeze by a construction site every time I use my back door?"

"That would be the case, but you know you can't leave anyway right now. What does it matter if we choose that spot?"

"Well," Claire bristled, "I'd certainly prefer to have some kind of privacy. It appears I will be under close watch for the remainder of this conflict."

"That is what it appears, yes," Moshe responded, rolling his eyes as only a teenager can master. "What game are you playing with me right now?"

"Come on," Claire appealed. "Talk to your Samal. We are hungry. We need groceries today. Let us go."

"No," Moshe curted.

"I am just asking you to talk to your Samal. I'm not asking you to invoke a Seren or a Segen, I'm just trying to find a way…"

"You may leave," Moshe interrupted, rubbing his eyes, "the day that Iraq stops using chemical weapons."

"I hear the Americans are purging the Iraqis from Kuwait," Claire augmented his stipulation. "This is good?"

"Yes, this is good. But we will see how it plays out."

Claire smiled, then asked, "coffee?"

Moshe angrily shook his head, but his lips betrayed his body as he responded, "Yes, please."

Claire crossed to the kitchen, but before she could grab another cup, the city-wide alarm just outside the Church of the Nativity began to whir.

Claire, eyes wide, looked over at Moshe and found him in just as much of a panic. Chileab barreled down the stairs from the roof, yelling "suit up!"

Claire exhaled as the two rushed out her front door. She grabbed a cup of coffee, then sat at her kitchen table, alternating her lips from sipping on her coffee to sporadically chanting prayer.

Zuji appeared into the kitchen once again, covered shoulder-to-toe in a hazmat suit, holding a gas mask at his chest.

"Claire," Zuji said, "I'd really prefer you put yours on. Even just once, so you know how to use it. What happens if we are under attack this time?"

"I love Him so much," Claire said, staring into her husband's auburn eyes, "and He knows that. And if the rocket comes and burns me up, then I'll be with Him. And that's okay."

"But what about us?" Zuji asked. "How could we fare?"

"Faith over fear, dear," Claire said.

Zuji sighed, then donned his gas mask. Claire gaped out the window and saw Moshe and Chileab both patrolling the streets, head-to-toe in the suit and mask. Claire examined the young men over. She could see Moshe was violently shaking, even visibly so under all the protective wear.

"I think I'm going to take a shower," Claire said as the alarms continued to pierce through the plastic-shielded windows.

February 2, 1991

It was a new moon. Bullets rang in Bethlehem, and Claire felt Zuji jolt awake at the sound of a distant explosion.

"Claire," Zuji panted, "did you hear that?"

"Yes," Claire responded. Of course she did. She's been awake all night, listening to the crossfire. "Aida Camp has been at it again."

The Gulf War ended almost a decade ago, but you wouldn't know it in Bethlehem, where Palestinians still sprayed Jerusalem nightly.

"Aida Camp has a right to defend their home," Zuji rationalized, as if saying it atoned for the unprovoked transgressions by his people.

"Maybe," Claire reasoned, "but Aida started this fight tonight. Before you know it, the Tzahal will be setting up checkpoints in Bethlehem."

"Hmmm, yet you wish to *stay* in Bethlehem."

Claire turned her head to her husband.

"Yes, Zuji," she said in disbelief. "This is our *home*. You know our agreement: the moment any of us become injured, we leave. Until then…"

"Yes, yes, that is the agreement," Zuji pined. "At first injury, we leave. I will stop bringing this up. But Saddam Hussein gassed his own people. How much more might an enemy do that to us if they acquired such technology?"

"Israel is wrathful, *not* evil," Claire said with confidence, then followed up with an assertion imbued with just a hint of diffidence. "They have never done this before, and they would not do this thing to us."

"Are you sure?" Zuji asked, capitalizing on Claire's anxiety. "Because if wrong, it will not be *injury* that we suffer first."

"Our enemies are humans, just like us," Claire reminded Zuji. "They take no more pleasure in…"

TCHUU! TCHUU!

More gunshots. Not from Aida Camp, but from the Anastas' roof.

Claire jumped out of bed and hurried toward the door.

"Claire!" Zuji called, stopping his wife in her tracks. "Where are you going?"

She looked at Zuji. He looked as pale as an American rendering of Yasue.

"I have a right to defend my home," she quipped, and fled up the stairs.

Claire reached the door that led to her roof, but it had been locked from the outside by the Tzahal on the roof. So instead, Claire skidded to her guest room to look out the window into the dark abyss of night.

Directly in front of her view, no more than 500m, was Rachel's Tomb. How she longed to visit it again, but she'd been banned from the site because she is Arab – despite Rachel being a matriarch for Jews, Christians, and Muslims alike.

The Tzahal had also taken over Hebron Road, the main street in Bethlehem, and there had been a strict curfew imposed by the Tzahal. When Claire looked out, she couldn't see a single person, enemy or not, but she did see flashes from guns light up both Aida Camp and downtown Bethlehem, of which Claire's window was situated directly between the two, giving her a full vantage of the fireshower.

As she peered her head out the window, a few more gunshots ring directly above Claire, dragooning the gun flashes from Aida Camp to turn towards Claire's direction instead of downtown Bethlehem.

Claire heard one bullet chip her roof, followed by a sound that sunk her heart.

Whiiizzzzzz…

Claire threw herself to the floor face-down and covered her head with her hands, but the rocket missed her house and hit the road behind her.

kpuuuh!

Bullets started spraying onto Aida Camp from several directions, including downtown Bethlehem, Claire's own roof, and from a building adjacent to Aida Camp itself.

Twenty full seconds into the onslaught, she began to hear screaming intermixed with gunfire at Aida, and Claire rolled onto her back and broke down crying.

"Lord!" she cried out, "I can't take it anymore! Save us from this bloodshed! Do not allow me to give into my cravings of fear, but give me a spirit of power and love and a sound mind! Send our people help! Send my family help! Please, give us an advocate!"

As Claire prayed, she felt a strange sensation come over her body, a feeling of warmth that started at the top of her head that traveled through her entire body and became cold by the time it hit the bottom of her feet, where the feeling grew warm again and travelled back to the top of her head until it pendulummed back to cold.

Claire stood in her place, all fear removed, then peered out her window and watched the steady stream of gunfire that had only intensified since her prayer.

"It is time for bed," she whispered to herself so quietly that she couldn't even hear her own words over the firing weapons.

Claire stumbled down the stairs, completely exhausted, and found Zuji in bed with the covers over his whole body.

"Claire, is that you?" Zuji muffled.

"I think I need to get some rest," Claire replied, then collapsed onto the bed and immediately began snoring on top of the covers.

November 27, 1996

"At first injury, we leave," Zuji reminded Claire of the promise she made years ago, glancing at her only sporadically so as to keep his focus on the busy road ahead. "*Fine.* But you don't need to throw yourself into danger, is all I'm saying. It's like, lately, someone has cinched your basic survival instincts."

"God will protect me," Claire responded. "Or, He won't. We don't get to decide that. We only get to decide to trust Him."

"And what happens when He decides to not protect you? Then our children have no mother."

"And at that time, you would get to decide to be happy for me that I am with Yasue."

Zuji sighed, and silence hung in the air long enough that they could hear a crossfire emerging in the direction of their house. Zuji and Claire glanced at each other with worry, then Zuji slammed on the gas pedal to get home.

Less than five minutes later, they were home, but there was no indication that there had been a firefight a few moments before.

While Zuji threw the car into park, Claire flung herself out of the car and into her house.

"Abni? Ebnahty?" Claire called out.

"Momma?" Abni emerged from his room, followed by his sister.

Claire hugged them both, almost knocking their heads against hers.

"You are fine?" she asked them.

"Yes, but there is a man on our roof," Abni replied.

"Yes," Claire responded. "Sometimes we will see men in those uniforms going on the roof, and there is nothing we can do about it."

"But momma, he wasn't wearing a uniform."

Claire and Zuji shot each other that glance again, and then Zuji rushed to the top floor. He turned the handle to the roof, which was unlocked. If it was Tzahal on the roof, it would be the first time they'd ever let the door remain unlocked while they were conducting operations on the roof.

"Hello?" Zuji called out as he slowly ascended the stairs into the full view of every sniper in Bethlehem.

"Yes, my sir," said a man dressed in plain clothes and carrying a camera on his collarbone.

"Who are you?"

"I am Marwan," the man said, flashing a badge. "I am with the media, a member of the legal press."

"How did you get up here?"

"Your son gave me permission, actually, after I knocked on your door."

"I doubt that to be true," Zuji said, flinging his arms in the air and then pointing a finger at his nose. "Who are you, to think that a 7-year-old has the authority to decide who comes in and out of households?"

"I am sorry. I got what I needed, so I can go."

"What did you get?"

Marwan whipped out his camera and showed Zuji crisp pictures of Palestinians holding rifles in the air as they pressed their backs to the outside of Rachel's Tomb, and a small group of Tzahal being mobilized from their military camp to respond to the insurgency.

"What is this?" Zuji asked.

"It is the new Powershot 600. No need to develop photos later, it can be shown in an instant. Just a third-inch sensor and over 800 pixel res on the width, auto white balance, and an optical viewfinder."

All of that was gibberish to Zuji, and Zuji didn't care to admit it to Marwan, but these were incredibly impressive pictures, and the camera unlike anything he'd ever seen before.

"I believe I am living in the future," Zuji admitted to Marwan, then quickly added as he remembered the gravity of the situation, "but you need to leave my roof right now. The Tzahal has forbidden *anyone*, even ourselves, from being on our roof. You have put my family in grave danger."

November 27, 1996

"It was an amazing camera," Zuji explained to Claire and the children as he stuffed glass noodles into his mouth, this having been the first time any of them had eaten all day, despite it being late afternoon. "I told him, 'you have brought this camera from the wizarding world.' He did not need to develop any of his photos, they were available immediately! He said that there are some cameras now that show your pictures immediately on a tiny TV screen that can fit in your pocket, and that…"

BANG! BANG! BANG!

Zuji froze in fear as he heard someone wildly knock at the door.

"Lehipatakh!" the person at the door shouted. "Lehipatakh!"

"Claire," Zuji said as a noodle escaped his mouth and into his lap, "they have come for me."

Claire stood up and began to head towards the door, but Zuji jumped in front of her and shook his head.

"This is mine to carry. You take the children upstairs."

Claire schlepped the children upstairs and they hid behind a corner couch. They heard a loud crash, but after a few moments, she realized she hadn't heard any commotion downstairs – not a peep from Zuji or the Tzahal.

"Stay here," she instructed her children and then hustled to the ground floor, where she found a single Samal standing in her doorway taking notes, but no Zuji.

"Samal, what's going on?" Claire asked.

The soldier turned towards Claire, flashing his rank. He was *no* Samal: he was the boss of the Samals, a *Segen*, only one grade below the top Israeli commander in Bethlehem.

"*Se-gen*," she fluttered a melody. "I'm sorry, I didn't see your rank at first."

"Shaket!" the Segen whisted. She knew enough Hebrew to know that meant "shut up," and she knew enough Tzahal to know that one does not become a Segen by pandering to his enemies.

The Segen took a single step inside the house and looked upstairs, as if he was thinking about going up there.

"While you're in this house, do not hassle my children," she instructed the Segen.

The Segen looked at Claire with incredulous contempt. Claire didn't mind him, and tried to get a peek out the door to see if she could spot Zuji.

The Segen grabbed his weapon, spun it around, and thrust the butt of the rifle into Claire's face, stopping no less than a millimeter short of Claire's nose – she could smell the carbon from the rifle.

"In some countries," Claire spoke into the stock, "Segen means 'blessing.'"

The Segen lowered his rifle and Claire retreated back upstairs to the western window to catch a glimpse of what might be happening to Zuji. She approached the window and spotted her handcuffed and blindfolded husband, just in time to see a Samal crack the back of his torso with his rifle's butt, sending Zuji to his knees and gasping for air.

Just then, another man was brought into Claire's view: it was Marwan, the cameraman from Claire's roof. The Samal brought Marwan to the Segen, who was now standing before Zuji, and he handed Marwan's camera to the Segen.

Marwan gestured his hands towards Zuji and argued with the Segen, though Claire couldn't hear what he was saying. The Segen ignored Marwan while he thumbed through the pictures on the camera. It didn't take long before the Segen had seen – or heard – enough, and he winded his arm back and thrust a haymaker into Marwan's ribs, forcing Marwan to the ground and into a coughing fit. They didn't need to handcuff him – he wasn't going anywhere.

BURIAL AT THE NATIVITY

The Segen pitched Marwan's Powershot 600 onto the ground, then spent almost five full minutes stomping it until the Segen's boots were stained with zinc and carbon residue. Marwan didn't protest, and could only look on with distinct sadness.

Claire's feet began to hurt from standing and watching through the window so long, but she knew it couldn't be worse than how her husband must've been feeling after kneeling on the gravel in the blistering light. Claire watched as a cruiser pulled up to her house. She sprinted downstairs, but before she even made it outside of her home, both Zuji and Marwan had been scooped and hauled away. She couldn't even see what direction they went, and Claire was left with no explanation of where they were going or when she could expect to see her husband again.

November 27, 1996

"You will be shot if you go," Okhti rebuked Claire. "You are out of your mind right now."

"I can't stand it anymore," Claire said while throwing on a light jacket, as the hot day turned to a very cool night without the summer sun. "We have been waiting for hours and nobody will even acknowledge that they took my husband from me. There is a time to pray, and there is a time to act, and this is a time to act."

"It is three hours past curfew, and if you drive to that prison..."

"Sister," Claire interrupted. "Will you watch my children?"

"Of course I will."

"Then it is settled. Please let me go."

Claire grabbed the keys to Zuji's jalopy and began the long drive to prison, knowing that an unmarked Palestinian vehicle like hers would likely be shot at.

"Lord, will You please send Someone to protect me and Zuji?" she asked as she drove into heavy Tzahal territory. Within minutes, she began to feel a warmth at the top of her head, the same warmth that she felt on the roof days ago. The warmth surged to the rest of her body, and when the warmth finished moving from one area of her body, it left a refreshing cool behind in another, and the rising and falling calescence flowed through Claire's body so fluidly that it felt like a massage.

Claire pressed her foot to the pedal and sped to the prison, where she boldly parked outside its gates and stomped her way to the front entrance.

"What do you need?" the guard at the door asked her, keeping his rifle pointed at the ground but with his finger on the trigger.

"My husband," Claire said, her eyes glowing with furor.

"He is a prisoner here?" the guard asked.

"I would like you to tell me that," Claire responded.

"What is his name?"

"Zuji Bishara Anastas."

The guard grabbed a walkie-talkie and began to speak Hebrew to the other end. He received a response in like, looked at Claire, and then nodded his head.

"One moment."

One moment later, a Samal appeared before Claire.

"Claire Anastas," he said, "your husband was brought here earlier today."

"Yes, this I know!"

"He has been released one hour ago."

"Where did you take him?"

"Take him? We didn't take him anywhere. He walked out the front gate, where you stand right now."

"You released him from prison *after* curfew, with no way home, knowing that he would be shot at for being out past 10:00pm?"

"This is not our problem. When your people stop shooting at us, then you will no longer need to worry about us shooting back."

"Which way did he go?"

"Where does any released prisoner go? Into the wilderness, I suppose."

Claire turned around, looking at the vast, barren desert behind her.

"You have no humanity," her lip quivered.

"I have humanity," the Samal responded, his eyes actually exuding pain by her words. "How am I to do my job otherwise?"

Claire felt her own disposition soften, so she retreated to Zuji's car and headed back home. There was no value in searching for Zuji: Claire was more likely to get bit by a viper than she was to find Zuji in that wilderness.

Claire crept into her home so as not to wake anyone, set the keys on the counter, and let out a deep sigh. Then, the hall light came on and she saw a withered, worn Zuji standing before her.

They didn't even speak. Zuji wrapped Claire in his tight embrace until she stopped weeping. Claire reached her hand and grazed her fingers through Zuji's hair, to which he winced from.

"Are you okay?" Claire asked.

"They blindfolded me and I tripped down the stairs," he explained. "I struck my head and became dizzy, so they carried me out. Come, let's sit down and talk."

Zuji pulled out a chair for Claire, then continued his story.

"Marwan, the man with the camera, he fought for me. He told the commander I had nothing to do with it, and a few hours later, they released me. 'What about him?' I asked. They didn't answer me and I don't know his fate. But at this time they released me, it is past curfew and I ask them to just imprison me until morning because I will not survive the night. I will be shot at a checkpoint or I will be stung by one of God's creatures. They refuse to imprison me, so I tried braving the desert, but it became so cold and I saw slithering animals. I turned around and begged and begged and they still would not let me back into prison. I asked if I can call you; they said to handle it myself and then locked the gate and left.

"I strayed down the road," Zuji continued, "and a truck passes by. I raise my hands and I think they understand how desperate I am, because they stopped, and it was three Tzahal. I beg them to take me to wherever they are going, and they say they will drop me off near Hebron Road. But when they drop me off, they drop me off at a checkpoint on the Israeli side. 'I cannot get home here,' I tell them. 'Please drop me off in Palestine.' And they tell me to talk to those at the checkpoint. I ask, 'shall I tell them of my story and that you dropped me off here?', and they panicked and said to not tell the guards that they helped me, and to instead just say that I hitchhiked. So, I approach the checkpoint with my hands up, and here I am, approaching a soldier after curfew with no logical alibi that I can use, and my face grows hot..."

Claire slapped the table, startling Zuji.

"You felt it, too," she noted.

"Felt what?"

"The heat."

"Yes, my face was hot. I was very anxious and in the vehicle we had many bodies pressed together."

"No, it was not body heat," Claire reasoned. "It is something else and I have felt this too."

Zuji raised an eyebrow, unsure how to respond to Claire's excitement.

"Claire," he concluded, "I bruised my head. That is why my face was hot."

"But then it was cold after? The hot leavened your body, and your face became cold, and your body was warm and cold at the same time and it was a comfort of peace?"

"No," Zuji said, grabbing Claire's hand. "I became hot, and, yes – the air was cold. But I approach the guard and he asks what I am doing and I tell him that I hitchhiked, knowing it is a terrible story that can't be true. He asked who gave me a ride and I tell him it was dark and I can't remember what he looked like, and the guard knows I'm lying and tells me I am under arrest and he puts handcuffs on me. And I beg him to take me to prison. I say, 'please, please arrest me and take me back to prison. That's fine!' And I tell him my story of what happened to me today, and he calls the prison, and they tell him it is a true story that I was there in jail today, though they can't believe I am somehow in Israel, but he lets me go. And I cantered the rest of the way with no more trouble. And now? Now I am home."

Claire exhaled, then leaned back in her chair.

"I felt something," she said, almost gasping for air as she spoke it.

Zuji shrugged, unsure of how to validate her feeling.

"The Lord was with me tonight," she said, staring off in confusion.

"Yes," Zuji said, squeezing Claire's hand and caressing her cheek. "The Lord is always with us."

September 27, 2000

Claire was changing the guest sheets – the Anastas finally had their first customer in several months, most tourists being warded off by the presence of military activity by Rachel's Tomb – when young Ebnahty came to her mother.

"Mama," Ebnahty said, tugging at Claire's blouse, "there is someone on the roof, and they are going pee-pee on our house."

So many things about that statement seemed off, starting with the fact that nobody had come through the house to get onto the roof, which had been locked ever since the debacle with Marwan years ago. Secondly, another crossfire had occurred between Aida Camp and downtown Bethlehem just minutes ago, so it would seem awfully bold for someone to be standing on the roof with so many opposing snipers about. Third of all – and probably the most important – it may be war, but this was a house of dignity. Nobody urinates on the Anastas house.

Claire hustled to the door leading to the roof and, after unlocking and cracking it open, listened for what Ebnahty reported. Indeed, there was a leak occurring, but it was much too hasty to be coming from a human. Claire realized that this leak on the roof was, quite literally, a leak on the roof: one of their two water tanks had been scuppered by a rogue bullet during the crossfire, and the Anastas family was going to lose half their already-sparse water supply if Claire didn't act fast.

Of course, it was forbidden for Palestinians to go on the roofs. To save her family's water, Claire would risk being jailed (or worse). But without that water, especially in the dead of summer, would be to lose their means of survival.

Claire headed back towards the stairs to see what she could scrounge up downstairs to plug the hole, but as her feet hit the top of the stairs, she heard an unnerving noise.

THWIT!

Claire froze in her tracks. She swiveled her head to look over her shoulder, but didn't see anything or anybody. But as she kept herself fixed in place, it happened again, this time louder.

THWIT! THWIT!

A bullet hit the roof, chipping away at the concrete on its edge. Someone was shooting at her. Were they aiming at her? Were they warning shots? She wasn't sure, so in a panic, Claire scrambled downstairs, slammed the door, and leaned her back against it and began to sob.

An untenable choice, and one that had to made quickly: allow her family to lose half their supply, or risk getting shot for plugging the tub? She could ask the Tzahal for permission to go on the roof, but by the time she received approval, the supply would be mostly gone. She thought maybe she could ask the Tzahal to mend her tank and refill the water, but they had already declined her requests for reimbursement after one of her windows was busted in a firefight by a Turai who had the marksmanship of a camel, nor were they willing to help offset her electricity bill when they occupied her home.

No, if her family was to have their water preserved, it was up to Claire to defend her home.

"Yasue," Claire whispered through her tears, "it is time. Please help me. I need an Advocate."

A brief, hurried prayer that culminated in Claire feeling her head as if aflame, followed by the brisk freeze of a silent, winter night. A spirit of fire and ice coursed through her body, and then she had an epiphany: neoprene rubber.

A few years ago, the Anastas had lost their water supply once before during a rare Bethlehem hailstorm that damaged one of their water tanks. They lost half a tank that night, and bought neoprene at the pharmacy the next day in case they ever had another occasion in which their tank chiseled.

This was that occasion. Claire loped to the closet, found two packages of neoprene still in their original packaging, and opened one package up as she launched herself back on the roof and raced to the tank.

As if they knew she'd be coming back, the snipers didn't miss a spank and shot at her. Claire heard the bullets pouring in behind her and in front of her, and she even saw a few spray in front of her face as the wind from the bullets slapped her cheeks. She thumbed the neoprene into a small plug, and sealed the hole.

However, she still heard water running and realized the snipers had added a couple more cracks in her tank, so she sidled around the cistern as they continued shooting at her, and she plugged each hole as they appeared, one-by-one. Seven holes later, she exhausted her supply of neoprene and realized she needed to grab the other package if she was to plug the last two holes.

"Woman!" a Tzahal cried to her from a distant roof. "Go inside! If we see you again, we will kill you!"

"What?" Claire cried out to him, cupping her ear to challenge him to speak up.

"Go. in. side!" the man yelled, punching each syllable as if each word was its own sentence. "I. will. kill. you. if. I. see. you. again!"

"I can't hear you," Claire yelled, amusing herself now.

The man pulled his rifle to his shoulder and peered through the scope.

"Okay!" Claire yelled, smiling and waved at the man through his scope. "I'm just going to get something!"

"No!" the man put his rifle down. "You. stay. in!"

Claire scampered down to her closet, unpacked the other roll of neoprene, and drifted onto the roof, eschewing urgency for accentuation. Bullets began to rain around her again as she ambled to the vat, keeping her head lowered and avoiding eye contact with the soldier. Taking her time, she corked the final two holes in her water supply.

No more gunshots. No more breaches. She turned around, descended back into her home, and feeling the fire and frost flee her temple, she shut the door.

December 30, 2000

Claire and Umi sat on the Anastas House balcony, each sipping their Turkish coffee on an unusually warm morning.

"There used to be nothing to look at on this balcony," Claire explained to Umi, "but now we get to people-watch every day. Even if they happen to be carrying weapons and are watching us in turn."

Claire leaned over the balcony and smiled at a Turai looking up at her.

"Hello, young man," she called below, waving. The Turai, unsure if he was allowed to respond in like, turned away and pretended he didn't see her.

Claire sat back down and giggled to herself. "They don't know what to do with themselves, Umi."

"Qassam!" Umi screamed, interrupting Claire and pointing at an object hastening their way.

The Qassam: a crude rocket created in Gaza that was propelled with common household ingredients like sugar and fertilizer, with the nitrate in its head exploding upon impact. It had first made its way from Gaza to the West Bank and, most recently and urgently, was now making its way to Claire and Umi.

Claire could certainly jump out of the way in time, but knowing Umi wouldn't make it, Claire stayed seated and chose to share whatever fate befell Umi, too.

Claire sputtered, "God will protect us," and the sensation of fire and ice descended upon her. She stared the Qassam down as it approached, and just as it reached Claire's property, the rocket's trajectory dramatically weakened, and as if it was slapped out of the sky, the rocket tip tilted towards the sky, hung in the air for but a moment, and then came crashing back to earth. It had enough momentum that it still hit the window directly below Claire and Umi, but its velocity was so weak that it didn't even crack the glass.

The rocket pounced on the dirt at the foot of the house and dust billowed around the crashsite while several Tzahal jumped onto a Sufa 3 and headed west, shooting towards Aida Camp as they seemed to pursue a ghost.

Umi dropped her coffee, the mug breaking into three pieces, as she bitterly wept. Claire reached over and rubbed her shoulder, but the consolation wasn't helping any, so Claire set down her own coffee and instead embraced Umi, who began shaking in Claire's arms.

"Hey, hey," Claire consoled Umi, as if soothing a terrified child. "Look at me. Look at me."

Umi kept her eyes shut, barely allowing the tears to even seep through the cracks of her eyelids.

"Look at me," Claire requested once more. Umi's cloudy eyes looked up into hers, spilling a backlog of tears down her cheeks, and Claire declared, "Fear not, for behold, the Lord is with us."

Umi leaned over the balcony to glance at the impotent rocket's final resting place, then she began crying again – albeit less violently – so Claire asked one

final question before enveloping her mother with her arms until the remainder of Umi's reservoir drained.

"Whom shall we fear?"

March 11, 2001

Abni and Ebnahty were huddled beneath their kitchen table, crying as they held their hands over the back of their heads, which were pressed to the floorboards. Their parents were fortifying the two of them with chairs, books, and anything else that could be used as a makeshift barricade in case another errant bullet came through the window.

In the weeks prior, fighting between Israelis and Palestinians had intensified as Arabs more readily had gotten their hands on weapons and often preemptively struck against the Tzahal. Once in war only by proxy, Bethlehem was now very much an active participant in the intifada, and on this particular night, the Israeli-Palestinian infighting had escalated each enduring minute over the course of several hours. It wasn't just the usual crossfire, but dozens of bombs had been heard going off around Bethlehem. The Anastas family had been eating dinner upstairs when the window cracked once by a stray bullet, then was completely shot out.

Claire clutched Zuji's shirt and pulled the both of them to their knees, then yelled to him over the sound of the explosions at Aida.

"Should we go downstairs?" she shouted.

"No," he yelled back, shaking his head. "There is way too much fighting in the streets. If we..."

THUMP. THUMP. THUMP.

A loud banging interrupted Zuji's train of thought.

"I think someone is at the door," Claire said, though it was hard to be sure that it wasn't a military vehicle turning over or even a dull explosion.

"I will go see," Zuji said, getting into a footballer stance and readying himself to bolt to the door, past the window that had been shot out.

"No," Claire cried, grabbing the back of his pants. "You stay here. Remember last time? You will not be going back to prison on my watch."

Claire scurried across the room, keeping one hand out in front of her face and one on the back of her head. She scampered down the stairs, hearing the door thuds grow louder as she approached.

As she turned the front door handle just enough to unlock it, a Samal flung the door open, knocking Claire against the wall as he sprinted upstairs.

Without a word, Claire lunged after him but was tackled by another soldier, who pinned Claire to the ground.

"No!" Claire shrieked. "My family!"

"Shaket! Shaket!" the soldier cried, then put his finger to his lips, urging her to be silent, as if anything she said could possibly be heard over the chaos outside.

Claire heard gunfire coming from the top floor, in the same room that her family was in.

"Let me go!" she cried, violently wiggling her way out of the soldier's grasp, but unable to outmuscle him.

She turned her head towards the door and saw bright flashes raining down from the sky – bombs or bullets or the sacred Bethlehem star, she wasn't certain and didn't care – and finally broke free of the soldier and hustled up the stairs.

Along the way up, she passed the Samal who was jumping down each set of stairs. Upon recognizing that he just passed Claire, the Samal turned and offered an exasperated cry of caution.

"Lech! Lech-Lecha!"

Claire soared upstairs into the kitchen and found that the sloppy barricade she and Zuji created had been tossed aside. She saw her two kids lying on the floor, but not her husband.

"Zuji?" Claire cried out, then approached her children and asked, "where's your Baba?"

But the children could not respond.

"Abni?" she asked, getting on her knees and shaking him. She looked into his eyes – or at least attempted to – and could not find his pupils, only his whites visible, almost as if they were glowing.

"Abni!" she cried and backed up in horror, only to find he continued to shake after she let him go.

Claire looked over at her daughter: her hands were frozen in a twisted position and the rest of her body distorted into angles that the most skilled contortionists wouldn't be able to pull off.

"Ebnahty!" Claire cried and then grabbed her daughter's hand to put them back in a relaxed position, but it was as if they were constructed of stone. Claire looked into her eyes to find that Ebnahty's pupils were also rolled into the back of her head.

Claire shrieked and watched as both her children continued to violently convulse, slamming their heads against the floorboards that they once were pressing their foreheads against.

As if Ebnahty was somewhere inside her own body, desperately asking for help but not knowing how to, she turned her head and peered towards her mother with pearled eyes. Claire looked at her lips and saw they were turning a ghastly Marian blue, and then saw Abni was experiencing the same fate.

"Zuji! They are not getting oxygen to their brains!" Claire cried out to Zuji as she watched her children die from suffocation as their elder sister, Mirna, had done shortly after birth.

"Zuji, please!" Claire cried out, but her cries were masked by a salvo of explosions right outside her home, compelling her to plug her ears with her fingers.

She unplugged her ears and found all the noise had stopped. Except, the bombings were still going on, she just couldn't hear it anymore.

"Zuji" she cried one last time, but couldn't hear herself anymore as the ringing in her ears became the only sound she heard.

"Lord, I know You are with us! Our Father, who art in heaven, hallowed be Thy Name!" she cried out.

"*Ask...*" Claire heard a voice command her, the only thing she could hearken.

"Thy Kingdome come! Thy will be done on earth as it is in heaven!" she continued crying, gaining some of her hearing back as she punched each word.

"*Ask for the Holy Spirit...*" the silent voice commanded.

"Lord, please send the Holy Spirit!" she screamed over the sound of the explosions right outside her blasted window. "Holy Spirit, I need You!"

Claire felt the sensation she had felt several times before: her head was filled with heaping warmth, and it traveled to her toes and back up to her crown, leaving a trail of arctic bliss in its trail.

Claire grabbed Abni's mangled, stony hand, and began praying in a language that she had never studied or even heard before. With her other hand, Claire grabbed Ebnahty's frigid palm and continued to pray in an unknown language.

An overwhelming heat – more fervent than she'd ever felt it before – shot from her own body and through her hands, and she felt it escape through her fingertips. Abni and Ebnahty's heads snapped back in tandem, and Claire felt their contorted grips loosen as she continued to pray.

Claire leered at Ebnahty, who was staring back at her with her sweet, pure eyes, her cerulean lips slowly regaining their natural strawberry color. Claire then surveyed Abni, whose eyes were closed but was now calmly breathing. Claire began to stroke his face, and he opened his soulful pine eyes.

The three of them huddled together, the explosions right outside their window seeming as if they were a thousand kilometers away. And for the first moment in many hours, they had peace.

"Zuji," Claire whispered, unsure as to why her husband's name escaped her lips. "Zuji. Zuji, Zuji, Zuji."

Abni and Ebnahty chimed in, quietly chanting, "Zuji, Zuji, Zuji," together. And then all three of them, as if rehearsed, coalesced to a thundering crescendo:

"ZUJI!"

The three of them heard a clatter directly behind them and turned their heads to find Zuji had fallen to his knees as a bullet spiked through the Anastas window, cleaved Zuji's frazzled hair, ripped through the bathroom wall, and collided with their master mirror, splintering it into fragmented daggers that chevalled back towards Zuji and drilled glass into his body.

March 11, 2001

Pieces of the Anastas shower curtain fluttered in the air for a moment, then floated to the bottom of their tub. Debris surrounded the Anastas family as they all lay prostrate on the floor. Claire poked her head up to see glass all over her husband's coiled body.

"At first injury, we leave," Claire remembered her husband say many months ago.

Claire rolled over to Zuji and began shaking his torso.

"Zuji," she said. "Are you hurt?"

"I..." Zuji gurgled, immobilized. An explosion down the street blasted through the street, then a few shots of gunfire, followed by silence for the first time that evening. "I... think I am."

Claire rolled Zuji over and began checking his vital signs, remembering what Umi – a former nurse – had taught her about basic first aid.

"Where are you hurt?" Claire asked.

"I... am not hurt," Zuji said.

"You just said you were."

"No. You asked me if I was okay, and I responded, 'I think I am.' "

"I asked if you were hurt," Claire rebutted.

"You did not," he said. "You asked…"

"What does it matter?" Claire asked, hugging her husband and crying into his armpit. Abni and Ebnahty both crawled over, and the four of them wept together.

"*Ow!*" yipped Zuji, then saw he had pieces of blood-stained glass embedded in his arms. As if he had done this many times before, Zuji began picking shards from his skin while speaking to his family. "But, why? Abni. Ebnahty. You called me *Zuji*."

He looked at them sternly.

"*Why* did you call me Zuji?" he asked, then added, "you *never* call me Zuji."

"I'm sorry, Baba," Abni cowered.

"No, I am not mad," Zuji responded, then plucked glass from his wrist. "It… *ow!*… it is okay. But I must know, you stopped praying together and then called out for me. Why did you call me by my name?"

"I… I don't know, Baba," Ebnahty skulked as her brother did. "I am sorry."

"No, do *not* be sorry," Zuji urged them again. "I stepped into the bedroom, right next to the bathroom, just to see if there was damage in that room. And I could not help but stand there in that room, paralyzed. But then I decided to come find you, so I returned to this kitchen, all three of you yelled my name. '*Zuji!*' you yelled. And I was struck with uncontrollable fear, and could do nothing but fall on my knees in awe. And as I did so, I felt a bullet over my head, then…"

Claire, Abni, and Ebnahty tried to gather what he was telling them.

"You saved my life," he explained. "You called my name, and I knew I was in danger, so I collapsed."

" 'Ask… ask for the Holy Spirit,' " Claire uttered.

"What?" Zuji asked.

"That is what the voice said. Ask for the Holy Spirit."

"Who is it?" Zuji asked.

"He is not 'it.' He is Him."

"Of course I want the Holy Spirit," Zuji said. "The Lord knows this already."

"Ask for Him."

"Yes, of course I will," Zuji responded, scratching his elbow. "May we be thankful that... *ow!*... that we are safe."

March 12, 2001

Twelve hours and what felt like a lifetime after Zuji fell on his knees, Claire was back in the bathroom, collecting glass from underneath the sink, where the waterline behind the toilet was leaking from an errant bullet.

"I think this will take many months to fix," she mumbled to herself in frustration. "And the Tzahal will not help us pay a single shekel of it."

"Hello*oooo*?" Claire heard someone faintly call through the opening that used to be the kitchen window.

Claire looked outside to find two women knocking on the door to her woodshop attached to her house, then hurried downstairs to greet them.

"Can I help you?" Claire asked.

The women startled, then turned around to see Claire.

"Goodness! You snuck up on us," one of the women said. "We heard that you had the best souvenirs in Bethlehem, and we leave the Holy Land tomorrow, so we thought we would come by and buy from you, and your sign said that you were open, but nobody was inside..."

"Do you know we are in war?" Claire asked, incredulous at their audacity. "Just last night, this area was bombed. I harvest glass from my bathroom floor today."

"Oh," one of the women shrugged her warning off, "if you are open, that's all that matters to us. We trust in the Holy Spirit, and He will protect us."

"Holy Spirit?" Claire repeated.

"Yes, the Holy Spirit."

"We are open," Claire quickly said, unlocking her shop door with zeal. "Yes. Yes we are! Please come in."

Claire stood at the register as she watched the two women pick up wooden trinkets, marvel at their craftsmanship, then put them down.

"May we take pictures?" one of them asked Claire.

"Yes, of course," she replied. "Please tell others about us."

The women giggled as they perused the shop, tickled by the interesting knickknacks they were finding. As most customers do, they had showed interest in many of the items, but ultimately came to the register with just a single artifact each.

"That is 55 shekels, please," Claire said.

They handed her an American $20 bill, and said, "please, keep the change."

"Thank you," Claire said as they began to leave, then blurted out, "who is the Holy Spirit?"

The women turned around, surprised at the question.

"You have not heard of the Holy Spirit?" one of them inquired.

"No, I am a Catholic," Claire explained. "So, yes, of course I have heard much of the Holy Spirit, and have received Confirmation. But to the extent of what you say, that the Holy Spirit would protect you, this I don't know about."

"The Holy Spirit – or, you said you're Catholic? Sometimes He is called the Holy Ghost, too," one of them explained. "But He is a divine power within Christians. A *real* power! And a most important gift."

"So He is a 'He,' right? Not an 'it?'"

"Yes, dear. He's a person. He has a personality, just like Jesus; just like you and me. Many churches don't explain the purpose of the Holy Spirit. He gets a watered-down overview, and most churches don't explain His role in the Church. We become baptized in the Holy Spirit without even understanding what the Bible says about Him. But Jesus wouldn't have been able to do any of His miracles apart from Him."

"Are you prophets?" Claire asked.

"No, no, *no*," one of them laughed. "We are Texans."

"I am a Christian, and I have a problem," Claire admitted. "I... don't know fear."

The two women glanced at each other, puzzled.

"That is a *good* thing, dear," one of them responded. "You have felt fear though, yes?"

Claire nodded.

"You know that feeling? The knot in your stomach? When you feel that, you know that you are not trusting the Holy Spirit."

"How do I know if I am trusting the Holy Spirit?"

"You will smile," one of them said, whilst smiling herself, "and you will feel the fire that can only reign down from heaven. And you will have peace."

March 24, 2001

"Yasue said that He would need to leave this world in order to spill the Holy Spirit upon the world," Claire explained to her children, trying to impart all she had learned over the past couple weeks. "Yasue was the harbinger for the Holy Spirit, who is now the harbinger for Yasue's return. Do you understand?"

Abni and Ebnahty, eager to please their mother, nodded their heads as if they understood, but their eyes proved there was still much confusion.

"I know it is hard to understand, but the important thing is that as you speak to Yasue in prayer, so you should also spend time speaking with the Holy Spirit, who indwells you. Many people feel like they're lost at sea when trying to discern the Holy Spirit, but..."

BOOM.

The earth grumbled, and several VHS tapes fell off a hanging shelf and crashed to the ground. Abni gasped and instinctively grabbed his sister's arm, and the both of them ducked behind the drab olive recliner next to them as the curtains whispered towards the center of the room.

Claire cocked her head and put her hand out towards her children.

"Stay here," she said, then jogged out her front door and looked over towards Hebron Road.

"Claire?" Zuji called over to his wife as he shielded his body behind the front door. "Do you see it?"

"Yes," Claire responded as tears welled.

"You see smoke?"

"No," Claire shook her head, "I see the explosion."

"Was it by the restaurant over there?"

Claire nodded, then added, "there is no restaurant there anymore."

"Get in, quickly," Zuji urged. "This will soon be a holy hotbed."

Claire loped back inside and locked the multiple locks on the front door, then sat in the recliner the kids still hid behind and began to weep.

"Oh, Lord," Claire lamented, "may today have been Yousef's day off!"

Claire's words hit Zuji as abrasively as the blast had, for his friends who worked at the restaurant were probably incinerated with the building.

"That was a kosher restaurant," Zuji said aloud. " Tomorrow is the Kippur feast. This had to have been the work of Palestinians."

Zuji closed his eyes, scratched his cheek, and shook his head before having an epiphany.

"They will be coming," Zuji said. "They will need their scapegoat. We should go..."

THUMP. THUMP. THUMP.

Too late.

THUMP. THUMP!

"*Potkhim!*" a voice cried from the other side.

Claire got up from the recliner while the rest of her family froze after hearing the enmity in the voice behind the door. But as she touched the handle, she heard a much different voice.

"Do not open... do not open that door."

Claire turned around and, seemingly speaking to nobody, asked, "no?"

"'No,' what?" Zuji quizzed Claire, who was as if she was talking to an apparition. "Open the door before he blows it open!"

Palestinians are required to open the door for the Tzahal, no matter the situation. If they don't open the door, the Tzahal are authorized to use force to open the door, and such decisions don't often end well for indignant Palestinians.

"POT. KHIM!" the voice behind the door cried out again.

Claire's hand remained on the handle.

"Do not open that door..." the quieter voice whispered again. When Claire realized it wasn't anyone in her family whispering it, she pulled her hand away from the handle.

"Claire!" Zuji whispered so loudly, he may as well have been using his normal booming tone. "Are you crazy? Open it or they will kill us!"

THUMP! THUMP! THUMPTHUMPTHUMP!

"Potkhim, potkhim, POTKHIM-POTKHIM-POTKHIM!"

The voice outside the door started to sound more crazed than angry.

"No," Claire said to Zuji, caressing his arm. "The Lord says not to."

Zuji walked towards the door to open it himself, but Claire squeezed his shoulder.

"Zuji, we trust the Lord."

Zuji's mouth gaped and the color in his face poured out, turning yellow and then as chartreuse as the recliner.

"Please, open it," Zuji pleaded with his wife, appearing like he was somewhere between physically-sick and already-dead.

"Relax," she disquieted Zuji. "At first injury, we leave."

Zuji's mouth remained open, and whimpered like he was choking on the heavy air, which now reeked of smoke and sinew.

"If they come in, I will ask them to kill all of us," Claire said, finding the most oddly comforting words she could find in the moment.

Zuji allowed a few disconcerting snickers to escape his mouth, though they sounded more like a sheep's bleating.

"Listen," Claire whispered, then smiled. "They are no longer pounding on our door."

Zuji stopped for a moment and listened. She was right: it was silent, save for the sirens in the distance.

"You're right," Zuji smiled.

It remained silent for a moment longer, at least until the loud ringing of automatic weapons sprayed the house. Zuji and Claire dove behind the recliner, shielding their children's bodies with their own as the shattering of glass rung upstairs. Claire looked out her window and saw lights in the sky, as if stars were plummeting to Bethlehem like rain.

"They're shooting out our windows!" Zuji cried, announcing the obvious. "We must open the door! It is the only way they might have mercy on us now!"

Claire twice tried to talk, but each time, multiple gunshots cloaked her voice. When the shooting stalled for a moment, Claire realized that not everyone was accounted for.

"Umi!"

Claire fled upstairs to find her mother sitting at the kitchen table, glass all over the floor, and the legs of the chair trembling along with Umi.

"Is it over?" Umi asked.

"Are you hurt?" Claire gasped, checking her mother's ankles for shards of glass, but exhaled when she found her mother unscathed.

Umi smiled at Claire, shook her head, and then simpered as tears sluiced down her face as if they'd been prevented by a dam. Claire rubbed her mother's shoulders, then felt Zuji's grip on her own as she bowed her head.

"I know what you're saying is logical," Claire reasoned with Zuji. "But I also know what God is telling me. And if God wants us to survive, Zuji, we'll survive. If not, He'll let us all get bombed together and we don't miss a minute with each other. We win no matter what is about to happen."

"Losing our lives is not winning," Zuji retorted, then squeezed Claire's shoulder again to offer tenderness.

"Yasue has said otherwise. We are already living as a dead family, stuck in this house and being slaves to the war around us."

Zuji whimpered and stroked his nose.

"Zuji... we have the Holy Spirit."

"Claire, what does that even mean?"

"He's an Advocate."

"We have always had an Advocate! His name is Yasue."

"Yes," Claire agreed, "Yasue advocates for us unceasingly before our Father in heaven. But we have another, right here on earth. He is completing the work of Christ until the return."

"Return of what?"

"Yasue, Baba," Ebnahty chimed in. "We have the Holy Spirit to watch over us until Yasue comes back."

"You know about this?" Zuji said, aghast at his young daughter's response.

"Yes," Ebnahty replied. "I have felt Him, like a jacket over my body."

"Zuji," Claire added one final point to her argument, "the army is gone."

Zuji perked up. She was right: they had been arguing so long that he hadn't even realized that the shooting, the pounding, the screaming outside had all settled.

It was the first time the Anastas family– or perhaps any living family along Hebron Road – had refused to open the door for the Tzahal. And it would also be the last, as Claire and the rest of the family would never again refuse to open the door for anyone.

"Let us pray," Claire said, bowing her head. And as she began to pray in an unfamiliar language, so followed the children as Zuji marveled at the natural flow of this language he had never heard before.

"Love," Zuji said, closing his eyes and bowing his crown, "I feel a hallowed heat upon the top of my head."

April 14, 2002

Only two years deep, and the new millennium had brought a generation's worth of fresh challenges to Bethlehem; events unfathomable in the 20th century. Hostiles increasingly targeted Israel, and the Tzahal and Palestinian insurgents were deadlocked in protracted conflict that continued to claim lives on both sides of the bank.

In one fateful clash, a group of Palestinian militants assailed the Tzahal, fled from them, and finally sought refuge in the Church of the Nativity. The insurgents took the clergy inside the church as hostages, and the holy ground in which Christ was brought into the world became a defiled battleground. The basilica was bedeviled into a standoff as soldiers, insurgents, and innocents alike were killed as the Tzahal pursued the aggressors and worked to free the hostages.

A strict curfew was promptly mandated, and Palestinians were only allotted a few designated hours per day to buy the essentials they needed – any Palestinians outside of their homes during the specified times would be assumed guerrillas and neutralized as such. Many families were too afraid to get groceries, preferring to starve than risk being shot. Even still, the lines at grocery stores in Bethlehem became so congested that it had become impossible to drive to the stores, grab rolls of toilet paper, and get back home before curfew started again.

"We are going to miss the cutoff," Zuji said, clutching his vegetables and milk in the line at the market.

"We will not miss curfew," Claire assured him, holding onto the figs and eggs with one hand, and Abni's soft fingers with her other. "Curfew does not begin for another hour."

"Maybe we should leave now," Zuji mused. "Perhaps this standoff ends soon and we have enough to survive until then?"

"No," Claire hastily responded, "this standoff has gone on for almost two weeks already. We cannot know when it will be solved."

"We should have split up again," Zuji lamented. "The bakery took too long, and now we will have no time to get to the pharmacy after this."

"We can visit the pharmacy tomorrow," Claire reminded him.

"I heard the Tzahal snipers shot one of the monks," said a Palestinian who stood in front of Zuji and Claire at the checkout line, swiveling his head to jump into their conversation.

"Yes, that happened a few days ago," Zuji affirmed. "I have heard this also."

"First they kill our bellringer, now they are killing our monks. Soon enough, they will start executing priests and none of us will be allowed to leave our houses after war breaks out in the Church."

"Believe me," Zuji told the stranger in line, "the Tzahal do not want any priests to die. That would make them look very bad."

"What do they care?" the stranger asked. "They already look bad. They have created gunbattles in church, throwing grenades in our most famous tourist attraction and starting fires in the basilica. They should just go in, kill the militants, and end this standoff for the good of all Bethlehem."

"Do you hear this guy?" Zuji whispered to Claire through his clenched teeth. "The Jews do not care. The Muslims do not care. It is only us who are losing our most holy place to violence."

Claire did not respond, so Zuji looked behind himself to find his wife kneeling on the ground with the back of her hand on Abni's forehead.

"It has gotten worse," Claire said, looking up at Zuji. "This is definitely a fever. We need to leave now and get to the pharmacy for this medication."

"But we have been standing in line for an hour, and we are so close," Zuji protested – at least until he looked into Abni's pained eyes and saw how unwell he had suddenly become. "Yes, we must leave now. I will put the eggs back if you will take Abni..."

"ATTENTION," a man on a military vehicle outside of the grocery store announced over a loudspeaker. "ATTENTION! I need everyone to listen."

The commotion in the grocery store ceased, and it became so silent that the only audible noise were the wind chimes right outside of the shop, which were picking up as the Sufa inched by.

"Everyone, go home."

As quickly as the pandemonium had settled before, the Sufa's new order stoked the shoppers into an aggrandized uproar.

"I repeat, go home. Curfew starts in *five* minutes. Anyone who is not home will be treated as a threat. Go home! Immediately."

Claire and Zuji exchanged quick worried glances at each other, then were pushed aside by the shoppers who abandoned their groceries in the spot they had been standing to rush home to avoid any chance of reprisal.

"Meet outside!" Zuji yelled out, raising his finger amidst the wave of chaos heading out the door.

When Claire finally made it out with Abni, she saw Zuji standing beside the Sufa, talking to the soldier on the loudspeaker.

"See to it yourself," she heard the soldier tell Zuji as she approached.

"But he is only five years old and so sick!" Zuji dissented. "Why can we not go to the hospital?"

"Two soldiers have been wounded."

"At the Church? The hospital is right by our house, if we can just get permission..."

"Not at the Church," the soldier corrected, "but at Rachel's Tomb."

Also right by the Anastas house.

The narrow streets of Bethlehem became the autobahn of the Middle East, the most inexperienced drivers suddenly becoming Arab Andrettis.

"Maybe we can treat his fever at home?" Zuji suggested, weaving through Hebron Road.

"There is no way," Claire said, shaking her head. "This is getting very serious very quickly."

"Is it better for him to be shot?" Zuji posited. "We have a much better chance of survival at home. We can get the medicine tomorrow."

"If two soldiers were injured right in front of our house, then, no. We will not be able to get the medicine tomorrow either. Besides, this cannot wait until then. I need you to drop me off at the hospital, and you go home and take care of the others. Abni and I will stay at the hospital until the curfew is lifted, or if it is not lifted, then we will sneak back home."

"That is too dangerous. Why don't I go to the hospital with Abni, and you stay safely at home instead?"

"Because I have a way of getting what I need," Claire said. And Zuji knew she was right: she was the shrewdest person he knew, and Abni's life was on the line.

After parking in front of the hospital entrance, Zuji lurched out of the driver seat and opened the passenger door for Claire, extending his hand to help her out of her seat.

"Go home and get some rest," Claire instructed Zuji. "Don't even spend a thought on me."

Zuji clutched his wife, laden with grief as if she had just been given a death sentence.

"You know I will not commit to a promise I intend to break," Zuji said, then kissed Claire on the forehead. "May the Holy Spirit be with you."

"And also with you," Claire responded, displaying her innate Catholicism.

Zuji crawled back into the car and watched his bride carry Abni towards the entrance, breaking Israeli law by sojourning after curfew.

"Claire!" Zuji yelled after rolling down the car window, suppressing his tears. Claire turned around and watched her husband's trembling lip.

"Love," Zuji pleaded, "you bury me."

April 14, 2002

Abni was asleep, his hands clamped around Claire's neck as they sat in the sanitized waiting room of the same hospital where Claire lost her daughter so many years ago. He was getting too big for this and the weight of his arms was cricking her neck, but Claire endured the uncomfortable positioning so he wouldn't wake.

On the television in the waiting room, the newscast was highlighting Rachel's Tomb, where the recent attack had canopied the next few days with an extended curfew. The newscast panned to a bird's eye view – being displayed by a helicopter that Claire could hear whirring almost directly overhead – and the Anastas guesthouse could be seen on the broadcast.

"Look!" Claire remarked and pointed to the monitor, forgetting altogether that Abni was asleep. "Our home is on TV!"

Abni opened his eyes for a moment, then fell back asleep. Claire was giddy – not from her guesthouse's fifteen minutes of fame, but from the relief in seeing that Zuji's car was safely parked.

Claire could hear the heavy sound of sprockets rolling on the ground just outside the hospital, then she saw the source of the sound – a tank – come into view on the TV screen. There was no turning back now: going home was no longer an option.

"How much longer, mama?" Abni asked, almost an hour after they checked in. He couldn't care less that his house on international television.

"I don't know," Claire admitted. "I know it's already been a long time. They must be very busy today."

Though it didn't seem busy. Nobody else was in the waiting room and Claire had seen a couple doctors laughing and cajoling the head nurse, a European nun with a beautiful face and a cute blonde bob that felt slightly ahead of the times.

Just then, an Arab family of three – father, mother, and son – walked into the hospital. The father was wearing a luxurious camel Bisht, while the mother flaunted a Harvey Nichols peacoat that still had its pricetag on – conceivably not an oversight on the mother's part. Though Claire couldn't see the exact number, the coat appeared to be worth four-figures in the British pound: worth more than most of the Anastas combined assets. Even the child was donning a Saudi Arabian farwa.

Claire looked down at her dowdy jacket – a hampered puffer coat that now looked more navy than its original violet – and moved her hand to cover the obvious tear in the left sleeve.

The blonde nun saw the family walk in, and before they even finished signing in, walked over and warmly welcomed them to the hospital.

"I am the head nurse here," the nun said in a soupy Swiss accent, "I have some time now, if you just follow me to the back."

Claire chased after the nun and caught her just before she had escaped behind the locking door.

"My son is very sick," Claire pled with the nurse.

The nun motioned with her hands for Claire to shoo, annoyed that she was preventing the door from being closed.

"Wait your turn," she said, slipping behind the door, Claire hearing it lock.

"My son has been waiting over an hour!" she yelled, pounding on the locked door. Getting nowhere with the door, she turned to talk to the receptionist, but nobody was manning the front, either. Claire collapsed into her chair again.

"Mommy, is it time?" Abni asked, his eyes closed and his head cradled in his hands.

"Almost, sweetie. Would you like to lay down?"

Abni put his head on his mom's lap and weaved his legs through the chair's armrests. Claire closed her eyes, and when she opened them again, she wasn't sure if they had been closed for a minute or an hour or a day, but she could hear voices coming back through the back door, so she leapt from her seat and got ready to meet the head nurse there.

"We'll send you off with the medications," the nun said to the camel-coated family as she held the door for them. "But, I'm throwing in a few extra doses, just in case. Thanks for dropping in, and have a safe ride home."

The father put his hand over his heart and gently bowed before the family cleared the room.

"My son is very sick, Sister," Claire stopped the nun before she turned around and left again.

"Your son may be sick, but you are playing with both of your lives being out past curfew. You are out of your mind to come here."

"And I suppose that family was sane?" Claire flouted.

"Refugees get the priority. You know that."

"*Those* were not refugees. They were closer to royalty than refugees. You chose to treat them, even though their illness was minor, rather than my son."

"If Bethlehem is to ever recover from this infighting, we must prioritize those who stimulate the city's economy."

"Will you please see my son?" Claire said, making a conscious decision to mind her tongue.

The nun sighed, then walked over to Abni in the waiting room and examined him as he sat there.

"This is a sinus infection," the nun said. "He needs antibiotics. Some fever reducer, too. I doubt you can afford it."

"I will pay whatever it takes. Sister, I also need a bed to lie down in. I know you have a guesthouse in this hospital. May I take my son there so we can rest until curfew is lifted?"

"Absolutely *not*," the nun replied. "Does this look like an orphanage? I am trying to run a business here."

"Perhaps you can let us stay in an exam room, or even the waiting room until tomorrow."

The nun's eyes widened and then began maniacally laughing, as if she was having a psychotic fit.

"*Woooooo!*" the nun howled so loud that her other subordinates came out from the back to determine if everything was civil in the waiting room. After nearly giving herself a charley horse, the nun calmed down and then calmly said to Claire, without even a hint of mirth, "there is no room for you in here."

Claire, feeling a fire come down upon her head – a much less calming fire that had no trace of coolness – spoke with authority to the nun as the other nurses looked on.

"You are a disgrace to the garb you are wearing, Sister. Why do you laugh at me? Because I am in need?"

"I laugh because you come here expecting special treatment. You are here past curfew. Is that my problem? No. You choose to fire weapons at Israelis, and this is the consequence upon your head. Do you even have the money to pay for your medicine?"

"How much do I owe you?"

"It doesn't matter. We both know you don't have the money."

It is true that Claire did not have any money with her at the moment, so she pointed at the television in the waiting room.

"That is my house that you see on that TV," Claire kept her finger angled at the corner of the room, refusing to lose her gaze on the nun. "I will go home right now. You can watch me on television like it is a security camera. If I slip into my house without being shot, I will grab the money and come back here and pay you. Please just let me have the medicine and I promise to come back."

The nun grew irate and began to say something that was sure to be pointed, until one of the nurses interrupted.

"Sister," the nurse gingerly interjected her soft voice, "I know this woman. She is an honest woman. If she says she has the money, then she has it."

"And I am to trust your word?" the nun scoffed. "I don't know this woman."

"Sister, if she doesn't come back to pay for the medicine, then I will pay for it out of my salary."

"Forget it," the nun replied, preferring to lord Claire's poverty over her. "I will give you your medicine. But don't you forget that it is I who am helping you, and not the other way around."

"*Help* me?" Claire barbed. "You do not help me. You have expert hands to construct such indignity from nothingness! I am used to this from Jews. I am used to this from Muslims. But you are most wretched of all, and subject to judgment. Where does my help come from? Not from Israelis. Not from Arabs. And no, not from Christians. You tell me now, how much is the medicine?"

"Forty nis."

"When curfew is lifted, I will come back with enough shekels. But you need to know something, Sister: we are in a war. It is a war where the good is blurred with the evil. I know this. But I also know that no matter who is right in this war, you are wrong, and you have stained your habit with evil today."

The nun didn't say a word to Claire, ordered her nurse to fetch the medicine for Claire, and the Anastases were on their way, weathering the one-mile trek to their house while violating curfew.

Claire lumbered towards her home with Abni draped over her shoulders as two more tanks started to turn off Caritas. Claire scuttled to an alley and squatted behind a dumpster, bracing Abni's head and shushing him from crying until the tanks were clearly a safe distance away. Claire hoisted her body and Abni's back up, then tiptoed down the dusty road, praying for provision as she inched towards her home.

Then she saw a red dot on her chest. And she froze.

"Hands up or we will shoot!" a soldier screamed from behind a barricade.

Abni began to wail, "please don't kill us!" as tears dribbled onto the dirt below.

Claire set Abni down and raised her hands. Abni, keenly *au fait*, did the same.

A Samal slowly approached Claire with his rifle raised to her face, bringing the count to two weapons aimed at her. Out of the corner of her eye, she saw Abni now had a red dot on his forehead, too.

The Samal approached close enough and, finally able to recognize her face, lowered his rifle and waved his hand down, snuffing the red dots into evanescence.

"Miss Anastas?" Chileab said. "What are you doing out here?"

Claire dropped Abni's medicine onto the road and embraced Chileab, sobbing into his shoulder. He had become so muscular since she last saw him years ago, when his post was still by her home.

"I... Abni came so sick..." she wheezed, barely intelligible. "I didn't know what to do. They were so inhumane and wouldn't help him..."

"Hey, hey, hey," Chileab said, patting Claire on the back as she held him. "It's okay. It's okay. Let's get you home, okay? It's not safe here."

Claire wiped away her tears and nodded, then collected the medicine off the ground as Chileab took Abni's hand and escorted the both of them home.

The Anastas family had just received more mercy from her enemy than her Christian sister.

October 17, 2002

The siege at the Church of the Nativity ended after 40 days, when negotiations were made to exile the offenders to Europe rather than stand trial in Israel. Even still, the curfew never fully lifted and it became a tiresome fact-of-life for Palestinians in Bethlehem.

"We won't make it," Okhti said, glancing to the back of the car where Claire's and Okhti's children were all asleep, all four of them packed together in the back seats.

"Yes, we will," Claire responded, stepping on the gas and feeling the pressure of the imminent curfew. "Can you try calling one more time?"

Okhti grabbed Claire's brand-new Nokia – her first cell phone she'd ever had – and dialed in.

"Still, nothing," she said.

"Don't hang up. I will leave a message this time," Claire said, grabbing the phone from her sister's hand. "Hi Zuji, it's me. We're on our way home from the birthday party. It wrapped up late. I will be home soon, but can you call me? I'm nervous that you are not picking up the phone. I love you, bye."

Claire sighed, finished down Hebron Road, and turned onto Caritas Street, but was immediately halted by a Turai. Beyond the soldier were a group of Jewish teenagers, all wearing knee-long kittels and spinning in circles as they danced to boisterous music as the clock crept past midnight.

" Okhti, what is the date?" Claire asked while the Tzahal jogged towards her car.

"It's... now? It's October 17th. Why?"

"The 11th of Cheshvan. It is Mother's Day in Judaism."

"Oh."

"Rachel Imenu is venerated today," she said, rolling down the window for the soldier to speak.

"You cannot pass," he said. "You must turn around and go home."

"That *is* my home," Claire replied, pointing beyond the soldier.

"I'm sorry, we have many problems today. I cannot allow you to drive your car near Rachel's Tomb."

"So the six of us must sleep in our packed car tonight?"

"Please just turn around," the soldier said. Claire noticed bags under his eyes so heavy that they might have left a wrinkled mark the next day.

"As you wish," she said, then backed her car out and headed back towards Hebron.

"What will we do?" Okhti asked.

"I have a plan," Claire responded, intently looking ahead.

"Which is...?"

"I will park and we will walk to our house."

"No," Okhti fiercely protested. "We will die. We will immediately be shot. They are not messing around tonight."

"Trust the Lord. We will be fine," Claire said, finding an abandoned lot with some emaciated dogs scurrying past her headlight.

"The Lord does not promise us such protection!"

"Yes, He is, Okhti. We will be fine."

"How can you know that?"

"He is speaking to me. I feel the warmth of the Holy Spirit. If you cannot trust the Lord, at least trust me."

Okhti sighed, but then was the first to open the car door and called behind, "children, wake up. It is time to go."

The six of them made their way out and approached Caritas by its side street. As immediately as they stepped foot onto the street, they found dozens of soldiers patrolling the corridor to Rachel's Tomb. And as quickly as they made it to Caritas, one Tzahal pointed them out and several soldiers turned their way.

The music from the feast was very loud. But it wasn't loud enough to mask the sound of multiple guns clicking.

Abni whimpered, and Claire turned around to find both Abni and Ebnahty a shade of squash.

"Are you scared?" Claire asked Abni.

"Yes, mama," Abni admitted.

"Then you're not trusting the Lord enough. He will see us through. I promise."

When Claire turned back around, there were four Tzahal standing before her.

October 17, 2002

It was almost a full moon, but the overcast clouds had shrouded any of the moon's illumination and Claire couldn't even see the faces of the soldiers in front of her. While the other dozen Tzahal looked on, three of the soldiers kept their hands on their triggers while one approached Claire close enough that she could see his face. He began to open his mouth, but Claire promptly interrupted him before he uttered a sound.

"I do not wish to catch your cold. Bring me your commander."

From the shadows, one of the soldiers stepped forward and announced himself.

"I am in charge. Why are you here?"

"Sir, I have been trying to get home since before curfew began. Nobody told us that we could not get to our house, which stands right behind you."

"How did you even get here? Everything is supposed to be blocked off."

"None of your checkpoints had any personnel," Claire said.

"That is impossible!" the Segen argued, though he knew full well that it was very possible given all the extra security that had been assigned to Rachel's Tomb.

"Sir," Claire continued, "I know you can shoot us and nobody would ever question you for it. Or you can have mercy, and escort us home right now and you will not have blood on your hands."

The Segen laughed, though it felt almost like a vulnerable laugh.

"Follow me," he said.

Upon entering the house after waving the Segen off, Claire called out for her husband.

"Zuji?"

Silence.

"Children, I know it's loud, but please go to bed, even if you can't fall sleep."

"Yes, mama," Ebnahty agreed, and the kids shuffled upstairs to their rooms.

"Claire?" Okhti called. "There's a couple voicemails here."

Claire pressed the answering machine.

Beep.

"Hi Zuji, it's me. We're on our way home from the birthday party. It wrapped up late. I will..."

"Okay, next one," Claire said.

Beep.

"Hi Claire, hoping you get this. I'm using Chauncey's phone, and couldn't remember our cell phone number. I'm behind schedule, and I don't think I will make it back by curfew. Can you please tell the Tzahal that I am being driven home in a red Nissan? I will be home in 45 minutes. Thank you, dear."

Beep.

"He called after you did," Okhti noted. "He must be on his way right now."

"Okhti, please tuck the kids into bed and watch over them. I need to tell the commander to not shoot my husband."

"Is the Holy Ghost telling you to do this?"

"No," Claire shook her head. "But there is no other way."

October 17, 2002

Okhti marched Claire's children upstairs so they wouldn't be privy to whatever fate was about to befall their mother for leaving the house past curfew. Claire opened her front door and was surprised to find a soldier with his back to her doorstep, who immediately spun around and shouted at her.

"No! Go back inside!" he demanded. "You cannot leave your house again tonight!"

"Boy," Claire said, tenderly, "how old are you?"

The soldier began to tremble, his composure crumbling at the first sign of Claire not cooperating.

"I am almost 18."

"You are almost old enough to be a soldier. Almost. Please get your commander."

The soldier fetched his superior, and when the Segen returned, Claire expected him to be indignant. But surprisingly, he was calm with her.

"Why have you not gone to bed?" the Segen asked, though it was less of an accusation and more of a genuine concern.

"My husband just left a message," she responded. "He does not know it is the day of Rachel Imenu, and he will be driving home in the next few minutes. I am begging you to spare his life."

"Hmmm. And does he know to drive slow?"

"Yes, he always drives as if a grandmother," she insisted, which probably would've driven Zuji into a fierce argument had he heard it.

"I will allow it," the Segen responded. "But there better be no tricks, or we will shoot. All 32 of us will shoot."

"I understand," Claire promised.

The Segen excused himself and spoke with a Samal, who promptly had all of his soldiers part to either side of the street and drop into the prone positions, watching the road through their scopes.

Oh, Zuji, Claire thought. *Please don't do anything stupid.*

Within a minute, a loud screech was heard as a red car careened down Caritas.

A couple soldiers strafed onto the street and pointed their rifles at the car, yelling "stop!" as the car drew closer.

Claire rushed onto the road and waved her hands, screaming, "Don't shoot! He's my family!"

The car continued speeding towards them, then in an instant, it jerked backwards and halted to a complete stop. Claire looked inside and found it was not her husband: it was a middle-aged Arab man with a girl, not even old enough to wear a hijab. Both the man and the young lady looked terrified, as if their lives were passing before their eyes.

"You know them?" the Segen asked.

"Yes," Claire lied to save the girl's life. "They're... lost?"

The car began to screech again as its wheels turned, and just as several soldiers raised their rifles to shoot, the car sped away in reverse and whipped back around the corner from where it came, as if a movie in rewind.

"Why did your family do that?" the Segen asked.

"I... don't know," Claire admitted.

"That was not your husband?" the Segen asked.

"No – he is in a different red car, then."

"Then who was that?"

"I can't testify to his behavior," Claire said, dodging the question.

"If your husband were to try to pull the same thing, then next time..."

The sound of a vehicle cut off the Segen's voice, and around the corner pulled a red Nissan, inching on the road as a pair of empty hands were raised out the passenger window.

"That's him," Claire said, breathing relief that Zuji knew to be cautious as he approached his home. "That's my husband."

The Samal approached the car, ordered Zuji to get out, and Chauncey slowly turned around and left after his friend was intercepted by the Tzahal.

"Go into your home," the Segen ordered Claire and Zuji. "This cannot happen ever again. If you find yourself in this situation once more, you won't be coming home. Understand?"

"Yes, sir," Zuji agreed, taking Claire's hand and rubbing it.

The 17-year-old soldier escorted the two of them to their home, still shaking from the whole encounter.

"Turai," Claire addressed the boy. "Don't shake. You are safe here. This is Caritas."

"We are in Palestine," the young soldier spoke. "There is so much danger here."

"Turai, who carries the weapons here? You're the danger. You're the one who holds the gun."

The soldier nodded, and Claire imparted a final urging for the soldier.

"Trust in the Lord. Be strong, as Joshua was."

January 6, 2003

Claire opened the door to her roof to find it still soaked from the downpour from last night. Earlier that morning, the sun's rays had finally broken through and the day was expected to be an oasis of shinedown before the weather snapped back to the rainy season by nightfall.

"If you go on that roof," Zuji had told her last night, his words echoing in her mind after she had detailed her plan, "you will be shot."

These words, in hot competition with the ones that came from Claire's mouth a few weeks ago:

"We are already living as a dead family, stuck in this house and being slaves to the war around us."

Besides: faith over fear.

Besides: women aren't shot at nearly as often as men are.

Besides: the kids need clean clothes.

Claire grabbed her bag of wet clothes and waded through the humidity permeating the roof to begin pinning her washed laundry on the clothesline.

What a beautiful white blouse, Claire thought to herself. *What a shame if Zuji is right, and my blood stains this.*

Claire glanced over at the watchtower, which was the only threat to her livelihood. This, in contrast to her balcony, which was in view of the soldiers at Rachel's Tomb, the nearby military camp, *and* the nearby watchtower – triple threat. She noticed the watchtower had a dirty window, hampered by the soot that came with the rainfall last night. And by the time she hung up the fourth of her five loads of laundry, she was convinced that the window must have been too dirty for the soldiers to see her. After all, she couldn't see any of the soldiers in the watchtower.

At one point during her fourth load, she heard two soldiers yell from inside the watchtower. And what seemed to be a mild argument between the two escalated to a screaming match.

My, someone ought to send a mediator for those two bickering!

Then, the window of the watchtower slid open and she found the two soldiers screaming at her: they weren't bickering, they were trying to get her attention.

"Are you talking to me?" Claire shouted across the roof, already knowing full well the answer to her question, but biding her time so she could at least finish collecting her fourth load.

The two soldiers climbed out of the window, shimmied along a shallow ledge, and hopped onto a small enclave that had a perfect view of Claire's roof. Here, one of the soldiers picked up his rifle and pointed it at Claire, while the other shouted at her.

"Go. Inside! Or he kill you!" the soldier yelled repeatedly, punching each of his words in broken English – the common language between Israelis and Palestinians.

"What did you say?" Claire shouted one more time as she grabbed her final piece of the fourth load.

"You. Die!"

She heard a mechanical snap – in fact, it might *not* have been the gun cocking, but it wasn't worth the chance, so Claire rushed back inside with her penultimate load of laundry. She crossed inside to the window on the third floor to find the soldiers edging their way back into their watchtower. Once she saw they slid the window shut, she grabbed her fifth and final load and headed back to the roof, quickly tossing each garment on a clothespin to dry.

As she sprinkled her family's clothes throughout the roof, she heard the watchtower window slide open and chuckled to herself as one of the soldiers sidled across the edge of the building again. When he made it to the concrete patch, he raised his rifle and shouted.

"Inside! Now!" he yelled, his voice cracking as he desperately sought control of the situation.

Claire turned to him, cupped her hands over her ear, and yelled, "Did you say something? I'm sorry, I did not hear you! I am doing laundry!"

The soldier rasped, "I shoot you!", losing his voice in the process.

"*Ohh*, okay," Claire said as she hung up the last piece of clothing. "I'll go inside now."

Claire returned inside and couldn't help but laugh as she watched the soldier have to shimmy back into his watchtower. A couple hours later, as dusk began to set, the final set of clothes had been dried and, doing her best Usain Bolt impression, Claire sprinted back across her roof, collected the clothes, and made it back inside just as the soldier had finished shimmying across the building with his rifle.

Claire watched from her window inside to see the soldier screaming inaudibly and throwing his hands in the air as he realized Claire had already escaped by the time he negotiated across the chasm. As he carefully treaded across the edge, Claire leaned against her bedroom wall and was transported into a laughing fit, winsome tears streaming down her face as she found herself crying from laughter for the first time since the day her dad had died.

"*Claiirre*," she heard a moan from the adjacent room.

"Yes, Umi?" Claire asked as she crossed to the next room, her heart crashing back to reality now that her frivolous escapades were achieved.

"Dear, I need my medicine and I'm too weak to get it," Umi said, looking directly at Claire, though her eyes didn't even seem like they were open.

"Of course," Claire told Umi, who really did look so frail and tired. Umi's wrinkled cheeks were stretched so tightly, her skin looked like a thin coat of cracked paint under those frail eyes.

Claire grabbed the pillbox on the dresser and popped it open, then wistfully sighed.

 "Oh, Umi: you're out."

 "I'm out of pills?"

 "Yes, dear," Claire responded. "Did you know you were out?"

"Oh, I don't remember. Perhaps..." she said, then deployed another moan that needled Claire's heart into a state of helpless compassion.

"Hold on, Umi," Claire hustled back to the kitchen to grab her Nokia.

"Okhti? Yes, it's me. Yes, everything's fine. Do you still have Umi's leftover prescription? Okay, I need you to open your front door. Leave it wide open... yes, please, just listen to me, it's important. Yes, everything's fine! I promise! Just open your front door. Hey, trust me, okay? I need you to chill out and work with me, okay? Yes... thank you, dear."

Claire cracked her front door open and leaned her head out to see how many of the snipers were in their regular positions. There was one across the way monitoring Aida. And then there were the two soldiers she just mocked in the watchtower, but their vantage wasn't great and she was fairly confident that they couldn't get a good shot off if they wanted to. And then there was the third, Behruz, but he's a good boy and he knows Claire and he probably wouldn't shoot her unless he was commanded to. Of course, she had to worry now that her antics on the roof had been called in, too, so perhaps it was better to not count on any goodwill she had previously built up.

She stepped a little further in the street and tried determining how quickly she could get to Okhti's house across the road. It takes the average sniper – what? – about seven seconds to get a shot off on a day with no wind? This day wasn't particularly windy, and Claire could pop over to Okhti's house in about 40 seconds. Should she zig zag? No, that would add precious seconds to her excursion.

And then all of these scheming thoughts came to a head when a red dot appeared on Claire's nose. The sniper from Aida – who truly wasn't even that far away and probably didn't need to be using his sniper rifle – had locked onto her.

Claire beamed a wide, nervous smile, held her hands in the air, and yelled "Excuse me, dear! I need to get something from my sister."

"Go back," the sniper yelled, assigning his words with authoritative clarity as he knew the wind might carry the echo of his voice away. "Go. back. inside. *right*. now!"

Claire remained frozen, the red dot cementing Claire's feet to the ground.

"I repeat! Go inside! Or I will kill you in one second!"

But Umi needs her medicine... badly.

Claire heard the sliding of a window and found the soldier in the watchtower – whom she had humiliated on the roof - poking his head out. When he spotted that it was Claire who the sniper was yelling at, he began yelling in Hebrew – or more accurately, a new derivative language known as Angry Hebrew. He tried to aim his rifle at Claire himself to shoot her, but his angle was so rotten that he knew he couldn't safely pull off a shot. Instead, he began yelling to the other sniper in English – presumably so Claire could understand what he was saying.

"Kill that bitch right now! She is making us into freiers!"

The sniper didn't shoot, instead first shouting to the soldier, "*you*, shaket!", and then yelled to Claire, "and *you*, go back inside!"

The watchtower soldier began yelling again in Angry Hebrew at the sniper, then yelled in English so Claire again could hear him, "Kill this bitch right now or I will leave my post and do it myself!"

But when the soldier looked back towards Claire, she had already slunk back inside, so he turned to the sniper and began yelling in Angry Hebrew.

Claire, with her back pressed against the wall in her foyer, exhaled sharply and said aloud to remind herself, "If you're scared, then you're not trusting the Lord enough."

Claire slid her body down against the wall and cradled her head in her hands.

"Lord, what shall I do? I have no way to get the medication. I need wisdom, Lord. Will you please protect me and send me the discernment I need today?"

As she prayed, Claire felt ethereal flame and frost come over her body. Sitting with the sublime presence for just a moment, she snapped her head back after a plan was hatched and marched to speak with her children.

Moments later, Claire was at the house entrance again. But instead of poking her head out, she pressed the intercom next to the front door.

"I'm ready," she spoke into it.

Three floors above her, Abni turned his head towards the back window.

"She says she's ready!" he yelled.

"Okay," Ebnahty said, watching the window. "The watchtower window is closed."

"The watchtower window is closed," Abni yelled into the intercom.

"Abni, dear, you don't need to yell into it," Claire's gentle voice broadcasted through the system. "And what about the sniper by Aida?"

"What about Aida?" Abni called to Ebnahty.

"He's moving towards us," she yelled over to Abni.

"Stay still, mama," Abni said.

"He's about to turn around," Ebnahty shouted.

"Get ready, mama!" Abni yelled.

"Abni, dear, remember you don't need to yell. It is very loud."

"Go!" Ebnahty yelled.

"Go!" Abni yelled.

At the front door, Claire winced as the words blasted through against her ear drums, then she cantered a couple steps into the street and, confirming the sniper was still walking the opposite direction, she gazelled to Okhti's house and burst through her open door.

"Claire!" Okhti blurted. "I almost closed the door! I thought you weren't coming."

"Please, Umi needs the medication right away," Claire said.

"Here, here," Okhti responded, handing Claire the prescription.

Claire returned to the front door and squinted towards her house.

"Ebnahty is giving me the thumbs up," she said. "Thank you, sister."

Claire raced back towards her house, but as if he had known her plan, the soldier in the watchtower flung the sliding window open and howled, "She's back! She's back! Kill her!"

Claire turned around and saw the sniper hurry to the edge of the elevated walkway he was manning and point his rifle towards the street, inspiring her to pick up the tempo and hustle into her home.

Slamming the door behind her, Claire leaned against the wall again and cachinnated so wildly that tears began falling from her face.

That's twice I've laughed until I cried today!

"Umi!" Claire yelled, clearing her throat. "I've got something for you!"

October 20, 2003

Claire stood at the sink, drying the dishes she had just finished washing. She felt particularly exhausted this morning, so when she first heard the bullets whizzing by her window, she thought maybe she was imagining them, at least until Ebnahty confirmed they were, indeed, thwitting by.

"Mama, it's happening again," Ebnahty said.

"Okay, kids, time to go upstairs," Claire said, as if she was nonchalantly trying to herd her children to brush their teeth or comb their hair.

The obedient kids marched upstairs. Less than a beat later, Claire heard pounding on her door.

Claire checked the peephole to see a horde of soldiers in front of her house.

"Open the door!" screamed the soldier in front of the line, startling Claire as her face had been pressed against the door and felt the reverberations from the bass in the man's voice.

Claire opened the door and found herself shocked to find that the group wasn't being led by a Samal or a Segen, but a *Seren*, the highest-ranking officer that operated in her corner of Bethlehem.

"What can I do?" Claire coyly asked.

"We need to get to your roof," the Seren dragooned.

This was a highly unusual request, at least given the time of day: in all the years of their occupation, the Tzahal never requested to use Claire's roof unless it was under the guise of night. This was the first time – and as she'd find, the only – that they wanted her roof during the day.

A female soldier emerged behind the Seren, nearly toppling him as she intruded into Claire's house, looked up the stairs, and announced, "We need to know where everyone in this house is, *right now*."

Claire looked at the woman's insignia and found, like the man, she had three bars on her collar.

Not just *a* Seren, but two! Two Serens!

"Oh, *my*, I didn't expect there to be two of you. I didn't even know there were two of you in Bethlehem! It is just me here, along with my children. My husband is at..."

"I did not stumble over my words," the female Seren monotonously replied, as if a robot devoid of human emotion. "I did not ask you to account for your children. I am telling you to bring me to your fucking children."

Claire knew they were in for it now. In her experience, dealing with female soldiers was the worst. Claire felt that female soldiers had something to prove to the men, and overcompensated by being meaner, louder, scarier, and much quicker to rash decisions.

Claire marched the entourage upstairs: both Serens and a handful of junior enlisted, altogether eight of them.

As they reached the top floor, the female Seren asked, "Which room are the children in?"

Claire begun to walk towards one of the bedrooms, but was stunted when the Seren grabbed her shoulder and pushed her backwards.

"Did I ask you to fetch the children, or did I ask which room the children are in?"

"You know," Claire cheeked, "in ancient Rome, it was shameful for a woman to wear a toga."

"What does that mean?" the Seren asked.

Claire remained silent.

"What does *that* mean?" she repeated, her eyes shooting daggers into Claire's.

Claire remained silent still. The Seren pushed Claire into the stairwell.

"Get on your knees," the Seren said. "And tell me which room to find your children. Do not call for them, do not move. Tell me which room they are in."

Claire glanced at her nametape, hoping that addressing her personally may de-escalate her animosity and help remind her that she is a human.

"Seren Alon, dear. My children are just through that door, in the bedroom. But I beg you: please do not be rough with them."

Seren Alon walked into the bedroom and Claire immediately heard Ebnahty screaming. Claire began to lunge forward, but the male Seren put his hand out towards Claire, motioning her not to move.

Abni and Ebnahty marched out of the room and were ushered into the stairwell.

"Fall on your knees, all of you," Seren Alon told the Anastas family.

The children joined their mother with their knees on the hardwood. Three of the Tzahal raised their guns and pointed the ironsights toward Abni and Ebnahty.

"Is this an execution?" Claire asked.

Seren Alon scoffed, as if Claire's perception of the situation was somehow absurd.

"I need to get on your roof," Seren Alon responded.

Claire's heart sank. The roof was inaccessible. Ever since Marwan gained access to the Anastas roof years ago, they kept the key on Zuji's body at all times.

"Seren Alon, my husband is at work, and he has the key to the roof."

"That is fine," Seren Alon responded calmly, much to Claire's surprise.

"He will be home soon," Claire responded, though admittedly, "soon" was a relative term: he hadn't left for work but two hours ago.

"It is fine," Seren Alon repeated, then added, "we will just bomb it open."

Abni screamed.

"Shaket!" Seren Alon barked at Abni, then took her rifle and pressed it against Claire's head. "*Shaket.*"

Abni stopped screaming and began to whimper.

"I will be back," Seren Alon informed everyone, pressing the muzzle of her rifle into Claire's temple. "None of you will move. If I come back and find you in a new position..."

She didn't finish her sentence, and stomped all the way downstairs with half the soldiers following her.

October 20, 2003

With Seren Alon gone, the room fell completely silent, save for the sniffles of the children. Claire closed her eyes and began to whisper inaudibly, the smacking of her lips shrouded by the sobs of Abni and Ebnahty.

"Yasue, Holy Spirit," Claire silently prayed, "I need You now. Come to my aid. Speak through me. Or if we are to die today, please have them take us all at once, so that these children will never know what it is to be orphaned. What do I say, Lord? Use my tongue for Your glory."

As expected, Claire felt heat at the top of her body, followed by the trademark chill as the polarized elements swirled around her body.

"*Ahim,*" Claire cleared her throat, then looked up at the male Seren and employed his name now. "Seren Vaknin, do you consider yourself a religious man? A real religious man, not in name only? Not just because you are Jewish. Are you a chosen man? A man of God?"

Seren Vaknin remained silent, opting not to respond to the onslaught of questions, nor would he even look at Claire as she asked them.

"Are you ashamed to answer me?" Claire continued her barrage of questions. "Are you not a religious man?"

This last pair of questions broke him.

"Yes!" Seren Vaknin shouted, almost with a twinge of pride in his response. "Yes, I am a religious man. I am a Jew! I love God."

"Do you have children?" Claire asked him.

"Yes," he replied, now with much more shame than pride as he understood where this conversation was going. "Three children."

"Imagine this," Claire pled, "that I would take your gun from you now and go to your home and point it at your children. What will you do with me?"

Seren Vaknin glanced down at Claire and found her wryly smiling.

"How dare you..." he began, only to find Claire's grin grow. "How dare you say that to me!"

"What would you do?" Claire repeated, demanding an actual response to her question.

"You'd never get anywhere near my house, because you would've been dead before you even got there, gutted twice before I let your corpse hit the floor."

"And yet you are inside mine, with three soldiers pointing their guns at my children," Claire continued, unvexed by the Seren's veiled threat. "I did not kill you, or try to kill you, before you came to my door. Perhaps I just didn't have the opportunity. But even if I had the chance to have killed you and your soldiers, I'd never have done it. Why, sir? Why would I not do that to you?"

Seren Vaknin inhaled deeply, then wheezed the air back out of his nose.

"I would not be able to kill you because, like you, I consider myself a religious person. Like you, my God is the God of Abraham, Isaac, and *Jacob*."

Claire let the words sink in.

"I belong to God," she continued her pitch. "And I do not understand, how do you expect me to allow you to blow up my house as you plan to?"

Claire continued to gaze at him, then saw his body loosen, Seren Vaknin easing into what almost appeared to be a hunched stance. Silence followed, at least until the front door on the ground floor opened and shut, and a stampede of steps thundered up the stairwell.

"I am asking you politely, now," Claire said, never loosing her eyes from Seren Vaknin's, "please leave. Go. I see your eyes. They are eyes that show me you are a man with a kind heart who seeks righteousness. But you need to prove that to yourself. But before you can prove it to yourself, you must prove it to God. And your moment is now at hand. You must prove it for Him, not for me."

"Everyone, vacate this building!" Seren Alon yelled as she ascended the final steps with a set of bombs in her grasp.

The Anastas children began to wail, prompting one of the soldiers to escort all the children down the stairs and outside their home.

"Are you not leaving too?" Seren Alon asked Claire. "Fine, stay kneeling there, if that's what you wish. But your blood will not be on my hands."

"So you will blow me and my house down? There may be no roof if you do this."

"Speak again, and I will tie you to this door first," Seren Alon riposted. "We have a right to defend Israel. And right now, this door is preventing us from being able to do just that."

Seren Alon slathered the paste on the four corners of the door, then slapped a C4 magnet to the top-left and bottom-left hinges. But as she worked on the next two corners, Seren Vaknin crept to the hinges and – without uttering a word – plucked the C4 off of the door.

"What in patriarchy's curse are you doing?" Seren Alon asked, snatching the magnets from Seren Vaknin's hands and re-positioning them on the door.

But without a word, Seren Vaknin pulled them off the door and tossed them to the ground.

Seren Alon grabbed him by the collar with one hand and threw her fist across his face with the other, a crack filling the air as his head snapped to the left. He calmly turned and looked directly at Seren Alon, but still did not say a word as a droplet of blood trickled down the corner of his lip.

"Don't touch these again," commanded Seren Alon. She picked up the two explosives off the ground and affixed them to the door, then grabbed two more magnets and appended them to the other corners.

But as Seren Alon plodded back to the other side of the room, Seren Vaknin picked off the four explosives again and dropped them at his feet.

At the sound of the magnets dropping, Seren Alon froze, tried to regain her composure, and then screamed and hurtled herself towards Seren Vaknin, only to be intercepted by the younger soldiers who held her back as she clawed to get to her colleague.

"Who changed your mind?" she shrieked. "I will kill them right now!"

Seren Vaknin held his hand out, "Tamar, quit."

Seren Alon stopped struggling as the two soldiers continued to hold her in place.

"You take your bombs," Seren Vaknin said, "you get out of here."

Seren Alon, whose face could've been confused with an overgrown radish, huffed once more and then stomped her way down the stairwell, broadcasting her disgust.

"Everyone, leave," Seren Vaknin ordered, and everyone complied, giving Claire a moment with the commander.

"Sir, thank you," she said. "Please, I have another favor to ask, and my hope is you're not void of altruism."

Seren Vaknin looked at her, as silent as he had been with Seren Alon, and beckoned Claire to finish her request.

"I have been trying to gain an audience with the commander who oversees this area. These home invasions, they are simply torture for my family. It is a living nightmare, and you can't imagine what we have been put through. I wanted to speak with the head commander of Bethlehem to request that our house be spared from these home invasions, as we have never stirred up trouble for your soldiers, and..."

"I am the commander," Seren Vaknin interrupted her, and then as if reciting a decree from the Supreme Court of Israel, stated, "The commander you seek an audience with is me. Your request has been heard, and I am granting it to be so. This will stand as long as I am in authority over this jurisdiction: there will not be any more invasions in your house, nor will any of my soldiers bother you again."

And as he promised, there were no more and none did.

December 17, 2003

"Mama, I don't want to go to school today," Abni told Claire, spouting a trope galled by schoolchildren around the world since the advent of formal education.

"And why is that?" Claire asked as she buttoned his jacket.

"It's cold. It's rainy. There's soldiers. And I just want it to be Christmas."

Claire chuckled at her son's innocently honest statement.

"But what would Christmas be if we didn't wait for it? Imagine if it was Christmas every day. Sometimes, we need to wait in the in-between."

Abni sighed, knowing his mother was right.

"Besides, Christmas is a week away. You don't have to wait long. Just two more days of school, and you can play all day, every day."

Claire ushered the children out the front door. The rain was piercing cold, and Claire winced as the droplets iced over her skin.

Zuji, wearing a thick jacket, scarf, and gloves, approached his children.

"It's all warmed up. Let's go," he said, rubbing his hands together. "Your cousin is already waiting in the car."

The children hustled off and packed themselves into the idling Toyota.

Zuji gave his wife a quick embrace, and seeing Arab contractors continuing to dig trenches in front of their house, shook his head.

"Traitors," Zuji said. "The whole lot of them."

"Stop," Claire whispered. "They are human. We don't know what pressures they faced before agreeing to do this job."

"They've betrayed our people. I would have never agreed to this, no matter how much money they offered," Zuji said, Claire's tenderness not allaying his contempt. "Do you think they'll ever finish?"

She checked behind herself and joined in shaking her head.

"I don't know. After two months of digging, you would think they'd have something to show for it. I'd just as soon have them dig until the day we die."

"Why is it," Zuji mused, "that Jerusalem is considered the world's most sought-after city, when it is Bethlehem that has been the central point of all the death from this conflict?"

Claire hummed, pecked her husband on the cheek and the entourage left for school. Claire was there to receive the group when they returned nine hours later, but she was much less jovial. Zuji pulled up to the house and saw tears in Claire's eyes. He didn't have to guess why she was crying.

The kids hopped out of the car and converged to where their street used to be. But instead of it being a road where they could play with their cousins who lived across the way, it was a wall. A tall, crude concrete wall that blocked out the light from Israel.

Abni sieged the wall and vaulted into it, as if he could climb it.

"No!" he screeched.

"Mama," Ebnahty said, looking at Claire, "there are walls all around our house. When will they take this down?"

"I don't know," Claire conceded, trying not to let her kids see how upset she was.

Zuji stood near Claire, mouth gaped open and unable to comprehend what he was seeing. What had been a valley in the morning was a mountain in the evening.

"This..." he said, "this is... nine meters tall? Or ten? At least seven."

"It happened all today," Claire said. "Piece by piece, they brought concrete and snapped the pieces together, as if a Lego."

"How will I get home?" asked Bent-Khalee, Claire and Zuji's niece.

Claire and Zuji exchanged glances. It was a great question: just this morning, she could've skipped a few meters and been inside her home. But now she was cut off from her parents.

"I suppose..." Zuji said, then stalled as he devised a course of action. "I suppose we must go through the checkpoint? And I will have to drive along the wall and find a street that goes near your house."

"Zuji, that will take hours," Claire said. "And you will need to go get a permit first to enter Israel."

"Well, we can't very well lift her over the wall. And I don't think they're going to let us build a door."

Abni began pounding on the wall, getting drenched by the rainwater dripping off the top of the wall and off of the rogue cables jutting out from the wall.

"So this is the end?" Abni yelled, the combination of tears and rain nearly gagging him. "It's not enough that we live on curfew? We must now be buried alive in a big tomb for the rest of our days?"

"Mama," Ebnahty said, "he is right. We have lived our whole lives next to the Tomb of Rachel. But now, this is the Tomb of Anastas."

Abni continued pounding the wall until his knuckles marooned, a massacre of the innocence for the well-mannered boy. Ebnahty wailed as she agonized with her brother's uncharacteristic rage.

"Children," Claire severed their fits, demanding their attention. "Look at me."

Abni dropped his fists and Ebnahty swallowed her grief. Everyone, including Zuji, focused on Claire. Even though it wasn't yet sunset, it was darker than normal as the wall behind their house was blocking the low-hanging sun.

"Hey. What does the name 'Anastas' mean?"

"Resurrection," said Ebnahty.

"That's correct: resurrection. We are a family of resurrection," Claire said, then felt warmth on the tip of her head that slowly trickled to the rest of her body. "You are right: we are buried alive. Our home has become our tomb. This is to be expected: when God moves, Bethlehem suffers. You know who else had a very bad first Christmas? Mary, Youseph, and Yasue did, as did the families whose children are buried at the church. Bethlehem needs resurrection, yet there cannot be resurrection without burial. When Yasue returns, we will not be excluded just because there is a wall. Yasue conquered the grave in Jerusalem, and there *will be* resurrection in Bethlehem."

"When, mama?" asked Abni.

"Soon," Zuji chimed in. "But, not today."

Ebnahty began to sob with Abni, and the two of them hugged as they wept. Claire allowed her tears to trickle, masked by the rain that was intensifying by the minute. Zuji rubbed Claire's back; he knew she was right.

"This is Truth," Zuji told his children. "Though we may no longer see the stars, we can still be the light."

The rain pattered the ground, turning the earth below their feet into a slopsink that could've easily been mistaken for quicksand.

"Holiness is pain," Claire reasoned. "It has been so, even since the birth of our faith here. Do we dare join Yasue in being light? Do we answer the call to be the light of Bethlehem?"

"Okay," Abni agreed, staunching the last of his resolve and tears. "I can do that."

"Me too," Ebnahty linked with her brother.

Claire nodded her head, then smiled through her weeping and answered the question she had posed to her children.

"We can be the light of this city, because He is the light of this world."

FALL ON YOUR KNEES
BURIAL AT THE NATIVITY

Claire Anastas can be reached at ClaireAnastas@gmail.com.

Burning Bridge Publishing
Copyright © 2022

Made in the USA
Monee, IL
27 February 2023